I0192468

HOLLYWOOD
Friends

by Ron Sellz

Co-edited by
Bud Seligson

Lost Age Publishing
—2017—

Hollywood Friends © 2012 Ron Sellz

All rights reserved. No part of this book may be reproduced or transmitted in any form or by any means, electronic or mechanical, including photocopying, recording, or by any information storage and retrieval system, without permission in writing from the Author.

Printed in the United States of America

Cover art and interior design by: Cyrusfiction Productions.

First Edition Paperback
ISBN: 978-1-946480-03-3

LOST AGE
PUBLISHING

9018 Balboa Boulevard
Suite #562
Northridge, CA 91325

SPECIAL NOTICE

A disclaimer is the act of disclaiming, renouncing, or denying of anything said or written by another person.

The following wonderful account written by Ron Sellz has been completely based upon his personal experiences and all comments and thoughts are strictly his own.

I have merely acted as his editor and added no comments or thoughts of my own upon any situation or person mentioned within this novel.

Respectfully
Bud Seligson

CONTENTS

FOREWORD
by Bud Seligson

Ron Sellz belongs to Hollywood and Hollywood has always Belonged to Ron Sellz.

Before we touch upon the many projects and successes of Ron, we need to know a lot more about that special place we all know as Hollywood.

Hollywood (informally known as Tinsel-Town), is a neighborhood in the central region of Los Angeles, California.

It is notable for its place as the home of the United States film industry, including several of its historic movie studios.

Hollywood was a small community in 1910 when it was incorporated into part of Los Angeles, California and became quite prominent as the film industry took off.

The name of Hollywood is now recognizable as a brand name known throughout the entire world.

By 1912, major motion-picture companies had set up productions in or near Los Angeles.

In the early 1900's, most motion pictures patents were held by Thomas Edison's "Motion Picture Company" that was headquartered in New jersey.

Any start-up east coast motion picture company, had to pay Edison large sums of money to work in this new and completely controlled monopoly of his.

To escape from his tight-fisted control, film makers began

to move out west where Edison's patents could not be enforced against them.

Also, and most importantly, the weather was ideal and the locations in and around the city of Los Angeles were perfect for background and close-up shots.

D. W. Griffith was the first person to make a motion picture in the Hollywood area.

His company which he called "The Nestor Company Studio," was started in a large road-house at 6121 Sunset Blvd. (which is now known as the Sunset/Gower Studios).

Griffith began shooting his first motion picture in 1911 and the industry never looked back.

Four major film companies were quickly formed and opened their doors for business within a few years, and by 1920, they were turning out moving pictures to an adoring public.

These start up studios were, Paramount, Warner brothers, RKO, and Columbia.

Practically overnight, Hollywood became the fifth largest industrial area in the United States.

Hollywood became known as "Tinsel-Town" because of the glittering image of the movie industry and its famous actors and actresses.

The famous Hollywood sign that is well known throughout the world, is not really located in Hollywood.

It is a few blocks outside of the official Hollywood area, in a place called Hollywood Hills.

It was originally a real estate development and the sign said, "Hollywoodland Not much later, the last four letters were removed and it simply became, "Hollywood".Over the years, practical jokers have altered the sign to read, "Hollyweed" among other things.

HOLLYWOOD

Friends

HIS NAME WAS BOB HOPE

On May 29, 1903, Leslie Towns Hope, was born in Eltham, London, now part of the London Borough of Greenwich as the fifth of seven brothers.

He was an American comedian, vaudevillian, actor, singer and dancer.

He was an entertainer and comic actor who was known for his rapid-fire delivery of jokes and one line punch lines.

He was successful in virtually all entertainment media and his decades of dedicated over-seas tours to entertain American soldiers as they fought in Europe during the second world war, endeared him to one and all. He was second to none.

§

No one is quite sure where the nick-name of Bob came from, but it stuck with him all the years as he grew up in Cleveland, Ohio, where his father moved the family when Bob was four years old.

Bob always wanted to be in the central spotlight, and came into his own as a comedian in high school, where he consistently had the lead in all the high school plays, and became known in a good-natured way, as the "class clown."

It was right out of high school, that he left Cleveland and moved in with a favorite Aunt and Uncle in Los Angeles, California, so that he could be near to Hollywood, where vaudeville was the hot item.

Vaudeville, as everyone knows, was live stage-shows that would feature specialty acts of songs, dancing, comic sketches and acrobatic performances.

Early on, Bob found his place as a master of the one liner or "quickie jokes."

He soon was working with other up and coming stage and future screen stars such as Groucho Marks, Charlie Chaplin, Buster Keaton, W. C. Fields, Abbott and Costello, Lucile Ball, and Jackie Gleason, to only name a few.

In his very early and formation years, he would team up with a much older and much more famous star of stage, screen and records, the singer Bing Crosby.

Together they would make many movies with the most popular one called *The Road to Morocco*.

This brought Bob Hope into the Hollywood spotlight which he never gave up until his death at the age of one hundred in the year 2003.

Bob is mostly remembered for putting together road shows to entertain our armed forces who were fighting to free Europe and the rest of the world from our enemies during World War Two (which was during the early 1940's.)

At that time, he became very famous for surrounding himself with dozens of beautiful starlets from Hollywood, his snappy one line jokes, and the golf putter that he never went on stage without.

Bob Hope brought a little bit of home to our troops who were fighting the good fight for the entire free world.

§

Bob Hope had three homes. Most people have one, some have two and a rare person like Bob had three.

He lived in Los Angles, Palm Springs (which is also located in Southern California) and the World.

My name is Ron Sellz and I first met Bob Hope as he walked along the main drag on the famous street called Palm Canyon Drive, located in the desert resort town of Palm Springs, California.

It was about one o'clock in the morning, and he had a few of his personal friends with him along for the walk.

All the tourists were back in their hotel rooms by this hour, and so it was easier for Bob to walk along one of the most famous streets in America without being molested by a bunch of autograph seekers.

If he had come out a few hours earlier, he definitely would have been mobbed.

Palm Canyon was like that.

The popular stores with all their big and fancy names were all clustered together for a few short walking blocks.

If you decided to drive on Palm Canyon, like a cruiser, then it ended rather quickly, so most people usually preferred to walk it.

If you continued walking down Palm Canyon, you would end up onto one of the parallel streets such as Indian Ave which was also a fun street full of great stores.

Indian Ave would then cut back to the original street you started on, which was Palm Canyon, and you were back where you started.

It was a perfect route and most people would do this path over and over again just in case they might have missed something that was going on.

When you came around the sharp connecting curve onto Indian Avenue, you would have to pass by a busy parking lot and a small free standing building that belonged to a local nightclub called "Jillys."

It was a secret known only to the locals, of which I was one, that Jilly was Frank Sinatra's personal body guard, and that this was his personal watering hole.

Frank Sinatra had a home in nearby Rancho Mirage, and it backed up to one of the many golf courses where Frank and Bob Hope often got together for a round or two. I never could find out who was the better golfer.

Bob Hope was famous for always carrying a golf putter around with him.

One day after I was better acquainted with him, I asked him

why, and he gave me a simple answer. "You never know," he said, "when you're going to find a game."

After that great one liner, I always smiled to myself when I saw him carrying around that putter. It became his trade mark.

As I previously stated, my name is Ron Sellz, and I was one of Bob Hope's most loyal fans.

The year was 1971 and I was attending the local college known as the "College of the Desert."

I would study each evening, and when the sun went down and the heat of the day faded away, I would come out and see my friends after we were sure all the tourists were gone.

We'd all hang out on the main corner of Palm Canyon and Tahquitz-McCallum Way, and talk and just joke around with some of the nicer locals we knew, and Bob Hope would hang out with us.

This was probably the greatest time of my young life. It was an experience of a lifetime just walking and talking with the guys and gals, and we had Bob Hope who would drop some of his great one-liners and crack us all up.

Bob was just one of the guys in those years, and whenever he was in town, he would walk the drag with us.

THE BOB HOPE DESERT CLASSIC
GOLF TOURNAMENT

The Bob Hope Desert Classic was Bob's pride and joy in the desert.

An amazing amount of major celebrities from all over the world came to Rancho Mirage to play a few rounds of golf with Bob Hope and some of the other big names that were drawn into the area.

As I mentioned, right next door to the golf course, you could see the fenced in Frank Sinatra compound, and the Wonder Palm Hotel which were back to back against each other.

The hotel offered completely separate large and beautifully

furnished cottages, for its guests, and Bob Hope, being the generous person that he was, always picked up the tabs for his guest's rooms, the never closed restaurants and of course, the drinking bars.

The tournament was the special once a year location, where anyone who wanted to see, and be seen, simply had to be.

And it was bob hope, with a great show of class, who hosted it all with lots of style, and the best of everything.

§

In the next year, I got a job at the Bob Hope Desert Classic Tournament of 1972.

I was the only person that they would allow to drive around in a golf cart except for the caddy's, who would be moving around in order to pick up the various players and move them along from hole to hole on the golf course.

My job was to keep the hot dog stands completely stocked with sodas, candy and hot dogs which were for sale.

On these special days, the movie stars and other celebrities could come out in force, and there were several thousand people around to watch the golfing event and see the rich and famous as they moved about.

The tournament was a tremendous draw. Jack Nicholas and Arnold Palmer were there and so was tennis star Arthur Ashe.

Even the Vice President of the United States, Spiro Agnew, was walking around on the grounds surrounded by his security detail. It was all very exciting.

You simply knew that something special was going on when you saw all those black limos and secret service guys guarding those cars.

It wasn't every day that you saw American flags on car antennas.

Please remember that the Viet-Nam War was on the minds of all Americans, and so naturally when Vice President Agnew rolled down his window as he left the scene, he was waving good-by to the crowd, but the only wave Agnew got back was a one finger wave back from the on-lookers.

Bob Hope may have liked the Vice President, but he was obviously one of the very few.

On this day in the desert, it would quickly rain and then clear up for a while.

When it got wet outside, a group of Hollywood Celebrities would all race into the bathrooms and primp themselves in front of the mirrors.

They would all hang out in the bathrooms until the rain would completely stop. Then they would venture out again into their protected world.

And again, it would begin to rain, and again they would race back into the bathrooms.

It was a truly a comical sight and one that I will never forget.

My additional job was to hand out from my golf cart, free coffee and soda to all comers.

When you are giving out free food and drinks, you get to talk to everyone, and I had the best of times doing so.

I had a great time talking to the golfers, the fans, the Secret Service guys, and anyone else who was around.

I was rubbing elbows with the very rich and the In-Famous and loving it.

I also remember another special episode very well because it involved Bob Hope.

The rain had stopped and I headed my cart over to one of the many hot dog stands who had called into our central office that they were running out of soft drinks.

There was a long line of people waiting for food and drinks when I pulled up. I know that I was a welcome sight for the workers who quickly took away all the food and drink items that I had brought over for them to give out.

To the delight of everyone, myself included, Bob Hope appeared and stood under the protective overhang and began to sign autographs as he handed out the hot dogs that were now ready.

Suddenly Bob Hope became one of the workers inside the

stand as I sat on my golf cart and watched as Mr. Hope served hot dogs, drinks and jokes to each of his admiring fans.

Then I saw something that made me sit up straight and rub my eyes. I thought that maybe the rain and the weather were affecting me.

I saw Bob Hope putting money that he received from the customers into his own pocket.

If they needed change he would give it to them from the cash register, but he held onto the large bills for himself.

Again, and again, I saw this happen, and being just a stupid kid, I felt compelled to say something to Mr. Hope. I couldn't just ignore what I saw and so I approached him.

"How's it going?" I said to Bob to get his attention.

"Hi Pal.," Bob greeted me. Obviously, he didn't remember my name even though we had said hello and good-bye about twenty-nine times since I've been living in the desert.

"It's kind of like this, Bob," I said. "You see, I've been watching and I noticed that you're taking the cash and putting it into your pocket rather than in the cash register."

Bob was taken aback for a moment. "Oh. You've been seeing that."

"Yep," I said.

"Well son, let me answer that one for you. Now who is this Desert Classic Golf Tournament named after?"

He looked at me and did not say another word.

Then suddenly it became crystal clear to me. Bob Hope can do anything he wants and I thought that it was great.

So, I answered back, "you're right Mr. Hope." I said nervously.

Then I took a piece of paper off the table and grabbed a pen. "Hey, Bob, do you think I could have your autograph?"

That was my perfect hole in one for the day, don't you think?

JOHNNY CARSON, BUDDY RICH, AND TONY RANDALL

Johnny Carson was born in 1925 and passed on in 2005

Johnny was known as the "king of late night television," as he completely dominated the medium's late hours for nearly thirty years.

He was born in Corning, Iowa but moved with his family to nearby Norfolk, Nebraska when he was eight years old.

He was the voice-over on *The Simpsons* television series and the television program *Cheers*, as well as *The Mary Tyler Moore Show*. What was unique about the episode was that the power was off in Mary's apartment and the set was black. It was then that Johnny Carson showed up for the party and we only heard his voice. Truly a great moment in television history.

He had a well-known clothing line called "suits by Johnny Carson."

He was most famous for the following quote:

"Happiness is seeing the muscular life-guard that all the girls were admiring, leave the beach hand in hand with another muscular life guard."

Johnny Carson trivia - Johnny Carson was seen by more people on more occasions than anyone else in American history.

Johnny Carson's trademark—a golf swing at the end of each monologue on his late-night television show.

§

Buddy Rich, drummer (1917–1987). Buddy Rich was known for his prodigious talent as a drummer and for his fiery temper.

His great career saw him work with stars like Tommy Dorsey and Frank Sinatra.

Born September 30, 1917 in Brooklyn, New York, this legendary drummer began his entertainment career as a child star in vaudeville.

He continued drumming until shortly before his death in Los Angeles, on April 2, 1987 at the age of sixty-nine.

Interesting highlights:

He was born in Brooklyn, New York, where he showed an early talent as a drummer and be easily followed his parents onto the Vaudeville stage when he was only eighteen months old.

He soon became known as "Baby Traps - The Drum Wonder Kid."

Rich performed throughout his childhood and appeared on Broadway when he was four years old, and he toured Australia at age six.

At one time, he was the second highest paid child star in the world (after Jackie Coogan), earning about $1,000 a week.

The speed and skill of Rich's drumming was absolutely astounding to anyone who saw him.

§

Tony Randall (February 26, 1920 – May 17, 2004)

Tony Randall was an American actor, producer and director.

He was best known for his role as Felix Unger in the television program *The Odd Couple*.

Tony Randall's real name was Arthur Leonard Rosenberg and he was born in Tulsa, Oklahoma.

While Randall played many characters in his long career, audiences remember him best for his role starring as buttoned-up-tight, Felix Unger, in *The Odd Couple* television program.

This program was based upon a Neil Simon play about two divorced men living together.

The show which ran from 1970 to 1975, won an Emmy Award for Tony Randall

§

If you are a lucky writer in the Hollywood community, you go through your writing career by yourself or with just one partner.

Sometimes it doesn't work out for one reason or another, and you end up working with more than one partner over the years.

If you are fortunate, each and every new experience is a pleasant and productive one.

Around 1980, I advertised in *The Hollywood Reporter Newsletter* that I was looking for a writing partner who had some connections into our community of writers and producers.

You see, it isn't enough to simply have talent. You absolutely need to know the right people.

Like the old saying goes, "it's not so much what you know, as it is who you know."

And so, I received a follow up call from my newspaper advertisement, from a writer named Mickey Rich.

Mickey Rich was older than I was, and the things he told me about who he knew in Hollywood was enough for me to agree to a partnership with him.

Mickey had worked for several years on the television show, *Car 54, Where Are You?"*

He worked as one of two assistant directors and thrown into the mix was the fact that his brother happened to be one of the best drummers in the business.

His name was Buddy Rich and he had played with some of the very best bands around.

He was also a frequent guest on many of the television talk shows of the day.

Buddy Rich had made several appearances on *The Tonight*

Show with Johnny Carson, and he was considered as one of the regulars.

Whenever Buddy would appear on the show, he usually was the first guest on the show.

He was a very funny guy and was very quick.

My new partner, Mickey Rich, turned out to be a great guy, and he enjoyed talking about his famous brother, Buddy.

He said that besides being brothers, they were also the best of friends and always looked out for each other.

One day after Mickey and I had finished the writing project that we were working on, he asked me if I wanted to take a ride with him.

He had to see his niece in Beverly Hills on some family business, and since he knew that I had nothing special to do, he thought that it would be nice for me to meet her.

I went along with Mickey and I was glad that I did.

Mickey's niece lived in a typical Beverly Hills home that you always were seeing on television or in the movies.

It had a huge front lawn which led up to her gorgeous house.

I almost expected Jimmy Stewart or Elizabeth Taylor to come walking out the front door. But, no such luck.

Mickey took me around the side of the house which led to the back yard. It was just as wonderful as I had expected it to be.

The back was as massive as the front.

It had a huge swimming pool and a large cabana which by itself was bigger than a lot of homes in L.A.

I met Mickey's niece and noticed that someone was swimming in the pool.

I didn't pay any attention to whoever was in the pool as I stood and chatted with Mickey and his niece under a shaded area adjacent to the pool area.

As we were talking, the man in the pool got out and I immediately noticed that he was a bald guy with not a trace of hair showing anywhere on his head.

I watched as the man dried himself as he walked over to a nearby table where he immediately sat down and picked up a tube of something called "sure-stick" with one hand, and picked up with his other hand what looked like a small furry animal.

It turned out that it was a hair-piece that he then adjusted on the top of his head.

Oh my god, I thought. That bald guy just turned into Buddy Rich.

Like the rest of America, in those days. I was a big fan of Buddy's.

But being on the edge of show business as I was, I was not allowed to show that I could still be star struck like anyone else in the country.

I had to act as if Super Star Buddy Rich was just like anyone else, so I remained very calm and smiled and returned his wave.

Buddy threw on his clothes and came over and sat with us at the poolside.

Buddy quickly dominated the conversation and walked us through a lot of his material, a few jokes and some comments. I remember him to this day, as being quite funny on that quiet afternoon as we sat around the pool telling stories.

Even though my partner Mickey and his niece were his family, Buddy was who he was, and he simply enjoyed being the center of attraction and I thought he was wonderful.

There was a lot of chit-chat and a lot of jokes bouncing around.

I added a few good ones that I had recently picked up and I absolutely loved it when I had the three of them laughing with me.

Buddy kept looking at his watch, and then asked me where I lived.

I told him that I lived over the hill in the San Fernando Valley, and that was when he asked if I wouldn't mind giving him a ride into the Valley.

"No problem at all," I said. "I'd be happy to."

So, after Buddy checked his watch a couple more times, he asked me if we could leave in that he had an appointment.

So, after a quick goodbye, Buddy and I drove over one of the connecting canyon roads, and we were almost completely on the down side of the mountain, when he shocked me with another question.

"Do you think you could take me into Burbank?" He asked.

"Of course," I said. "What's in Burbank?"

NBC, he answered. I'm on *The Tonight Show*."

Oh my God, I thought to myself. Buddy Rich who is sitting in my car, is going to be on the Johnny Carson show. Oh my God.

I acted nonchalant, as Buddy Rich and I drove to NBC in a 1978 beat-up Dodge Aspen station wagon.

I was kind of embarrassed that I was taking Buddy Rich to see Johnny Carson in such a crummy car.

But, I decided, it didn't really matter because no one would see me.

When we got to the NBC studios, Buddy directed me to a side gate where a security guard came up to the car and looked at us.

As soon as he saw Buddy, he had the wooden gate raised and I drove onto the lot. I REALLY FELT LIKE A BIG SHOT.

"What are you going to do after you drop me off?" Buddy asked.

"Nothing special," was my response.

"Do you want to stay and watch the show, only this time you'll see it from the inside looking out."

"Sure," I answered calmly. "Be calm," I said to myself, "just act cool."

§

Buddy had me drive around to the side of the huge main building.

"Park there," he said.

I did not mind parking where he pointed because I would then be parked right next to a brand new white Corvette.

When I got out of my car, I noticed a sign in front of the white Corvette. It read Johnny Carson.

Oh, my god, I thought. *I'm parked next to Johnny Carson.*

Outside of watching Johnny Carson perform at the Sahara

Hotel in Las Vegas, this was the closest I've ever been to one of my all-time favorite celebrities.

Johnny Carson, of course, was way bigger and much more important than my new friend Buddy Rich, and I knew that with the two of them, I still had to act nonchalant.

I had to pretend that meeting important people was an everyday thing for me.

I followed Buddy into the building and down a long hallway.

We stopped and then entered a door that actually had Buddy's name on it.

Buddy's dressing room was like a small apartment in the city. It had everything in it including a full kitchen with a garbage disposal.

Buddy told me to make myself comfortable and I did.

I sat down on the couch and phoned one of the writers on the show who I knew.

I had met writer Jim Mulholland for lunch one day not too long ago. Our mutual interest was the famous comedy team, Abbott and Costello.

I had spent a great deal of time visiting Bud Abbott at his house, and I knew Lou Costello's daughter, Carole.

Carole and I were writing a history of the comedy team. She had all of Costello's things from his career.

My friend Jim Mulholland wrote a book a few years earlier about the great comedy team, and it was interesting when he told me that I should have been the one to have written that book, since he believed I knew more about the famous duo than he did.

I just laughed off Jim's comments, but I secretly felt that he was right.

Anyway, as I was talking to Jim, it occurred to me that I had something I forgot to ask Buddy.

So I ended my call with Jim and waited for Buddy to finish up his telephone conversation.

"Hey Buddy. You're a good friend of Johnny Carson, aren't you?"

"Sure kid."

"Well, since you and Johnny are such good friends, don't you visit Johnny before the show"?

"Oh no," Buddy answered. "I never bug Johnny before the show. He's got a few million things to do before he goes on the air.

So now I knew that I could relax and not worry about meeting Johnny Carson.

I lied down on the couch, lit up a cigarette and stretched out. After all, Buddy's dressing room was big enough for both of us, and I was his invited guest.

Suddenly, there was a few quick knocks on the door, and it opened before anyone could get to it.

I recognized him right away from the show. He was one of the main members of The Tonight Show Band.

"Hey Buddy," he asked. "You got any pot in here?"

"No I don't. Buddy quickly answered as he glanced over at me.

"Okay." The man said and he left.

That was pretty neat to see a band member, I thought. He's one of several guys that Johnny liked to joke around with.

There was a table in front of the couch which had a plastic box of loose cigarettes inside.

"Hey kid," Buddy said. "Can I have one of your smokes? I hate those stale cigarettes that they leave around here for us to smoke."

In those days, no one thought anything about smoking, because almost everyone did it, or maybe it just seemed that way to me.

I gave Buddy one of my Camel cigarettes. Everyone always borrowed cigarettes from everyone else, and in the end, it all evened out.

Even Johnny Carson smoked while on the air doing his show.

Cigarettes were everywhere.

Another knock on the door and Buddy answered.

It was the same band member, and he had a couple of joints for Buddy.

Buddy asked him to stay, but he begged off. "Have a good

time with the joints. They're really good stuff."

As he left, I couldn't help but think that any pot that comes from a member of the band had to be *great stuff.*

Buddy lit a joint and handed it to me as he lit the second one. I took a couple of puffs and could feel the smoke coursing through my body.

This is great, I thought. What a way to end my day.

I took another puff as the door opened and Johnny Carson himself entered the dressing room.

He was wearing his slacks, tee shirt and make-up scarf.

Johnny sniffed around, but did not say anything.

I stood up, but I didn't know what to do with the joint that I was holding.

I didn't see what Buddy did with his so I could follow his actions, so I cupped the joint in my left hand as Buddy introduced me to Johnny.

Not knowing what else to do, I slipped the lit joint into my pants pocket.

As I shook hands with Johnny, I couldn't see his face because Buddy was standing between us.

I was very nervous and my pants pocket was getting pretty hot, but for some reason (probably the joint I had just puffed) I felt a joke coming on.

"So," I said to Johnny, "You sound a lot like Rich Little (for those of you that are too young to know who Rich Little was, he was noted for his voiced impersonations of famous people and Johnny Carson was one of his favorite voices.)

Johnny chuckled at my Rich Little joke and said to me with a big smile on his face, "I'll make the jokes around here," and we all laughed for a moment.

Johnny said his goodbyes and left the room.

It was just in time because my pocket was beginning to sizzle.

"I thought you said that you don't see Johnny before the show."

"I did say that," Buddy said. "But I didn't say anything about Johnny coming to visit me."

Buddy seemed to get a kick out of watching me squirm a bit.

After we finished getting high, Buddy started getting dressed for the show.

"Are you playing the drums tonight?" I asked.

"Kid, they don't have me here for my good looks."

It was then that I realized what I had heard my whole life about musicians. They really do get stoned before they give a performance.

Looking back as I often do, I realized that Buddy was not the best example of the music industry, but I had never met a musician before and he did get the marijuana from one of his fellow musicians. So, my opinion somewhat was formed by the facts.

We headed for the stage, and the closer we got, the louder the band got.

We must have been really close because I could clearly hear Johnny's voice doing the monologue as we came through the side curtain and headed for the audience seats.

We passed those seats and Buddy told me to keep going so that I could watch the show from the little room behind the auditorium seats called the green room.

Buddy walked me to the door and as I went in he turned and left.

Before I stepped into the green room, I turned and saw a great view of the stage, the audience and all of the television cameras.

Buddy was Johnny's first guest, and they had a lot of fun joking back and forth.

I couldn't help thinking that Buddy was stoned, and I wondered if Johnny was a little high from hanging out in our dressing room for a few minutes, but Johnny did not appear to be.

He was always sharp as a tack, and when Buddy went over to join the band and play the drums, I headed into the green room and saw that it was already occupied.

It was Tony Randall who was waiting.

Tony was a huge star from stage and screen as well as television. I knew him as playing Felix Unger in *"The Odd Couple."*

I introduced myself to him, and we shared a table in front of a television monitor.

Tony seemed to be very nervous, but I figured that it was because he would be going on the show in a few minutes, and it was a natural thing to be nervous.

On a show like this, you never know what's going to happen, but with Johnny Carson, everyone knew that they were always in good hands.

Johnny always made sure that his guests looked good.

This was unlike a lot of today's talk show hosts that only care about themselves and how they looked in front of the camera.

As we sat there, Tony Randall was fidgeting. His fingers were always being in constant motion. He kept tapping the table again and again.

He nervously would let his fingers fly across the table in a back and forth motion.

I don't think that my smoking a cigarette in front of him helped him with his nervousness. After all I knew that he was a big non-smoking advocate.

I saw how much my smoking bothered him, but I just continued until he just had to say something to me.

"Why do you do that. Why do you have to smoke?"

"I love smoking," I answered.

"You shouldn't do that," he continued to say, "How would you like to see a picture of your lungs with all that smoke inside of you?"

Fortunately, at that moment, Tony Randall was summoned from the green room and went directly on stage.

I knew that I had upset him, but he was a professional, and he wouldn't let it show during his time on the program.

I guess I kind of pissed him off on purpose, because it was easy. As mean as that might sound, I had a lot of fun doing it, and I'd never have that chance again so I took it.

A few years later Tony Randall passed away and I was sad that I could not tell him that I had given up smoking because of him.

JOHN TRAVOLTA

John Travolta (born February 18, 1954) is an American actor, dancer and singer.

Travolta first became known in the 1970's, after appearing on the television series *Welcome Back Kotter* (1975–1979), and starring in the box office success '*Saturday Night Fever*' (1977) and *Grease* (1978).

His acting career declined through the 1980's, but enjoyed a resurgence in the 1990's with his role in *Pulp Fiction* (1994).

He has since starred in films such as *Face/Off* (1997), *Swordfish* (2001), *Wild Hogs* and *Hairspray* (both 2007)

Travolta was nominated for the "Academy Award for Best Actor" for performances in *Saturday Night Fever* and *Pulp Fiction*.

He won his only "Golden Globe Award for Best Picture"-musical or comedy for his performance in *Get Shorty*, and has received a total of six nominations, with the most recent being in the year 2008.

Travolta received his first two "Emmy" awards as producer and actor for his portrayal of lawyer Robert Shapiro in *The People vs. O. J. Simpson*.

He received an "FX True Crime Anthology Series Award for American Crime Stories." In 2014, he received the "IIFA Award for Outstanding Achievement in International Cinema."

Among his many other accomplishments, John Travolta is an accomplished private plane pilot and he was applauded in 2010 for flying his private plane into Haiti during their disaster, when he brought them medical supplies, doctors and volunteers.

Overall, John Travolta seems to be a very good person

—Ron Sellz

§

Calling John Travolta, a friend is a real stretch of the imagination for me.

I had gotten a job at ABC Studios as the head writer on an ABC special where I was under contract for six wonderful months.

The studio always would allow the six-month time frame so that a one hour special could be completed from start to finish with nothing hanging over.

The studio on Prospect Avenue in Hollywood was a great big playground for me.

At that time, ABC was shooting two main-line shows there. They were *Welcome Back Kotter* and *Soap* which were both comedies.

Since I was the writer with the most screen credits, I got to pick my own office on the special third floor.

It was an absolute writer's dream office.

I had the biggest office on the floor and a connecting smaller one for my personal secretary.

It was the perfect set-up. It was like having a two-bedroom apartment with an additional guest bedroom.

I had a television set which connected directly to whatever was being filmed or rehearsed.

The only show I couldn't ever get into was the other comedy show, *Soap*.

This show was filmed in secrecy, and I couldn't even get onto the adjacent sound stage even though I was working next door.

There was a special security guard on the main door who only would let people in who actually worked on the show.

My very best 'bull-shit' did not work on this guard who

was really dedicated and very careful who went in and out of his locked location.

When I wasn't writing in my own office, I liked to watch the action on my direct television connection to the *Welcome Back Kotter* set.

And in that way, I saw John Travolta rehearsing with the other actors and I screamed and shouted at the television set as I watched him screwing up his written lines. How difficult was it to read sentences from a hand-held script?

On the show itself, he played a kind of stupid acting pretty boy, and I noted that on the set and off the shooting screen, he seemed to be pretty sloppy like his character.

I thought that he was just screwing around at first, but after a while, I could see that it was not an act. He just didn't bother to learn his lines.

Welcome Back Kotter was a show about a teacher who returns to the school he attended when he was a student, and he has to contend with a likeable group of misfits referred to as "Sweat Hogs."

Gabe Kaplan who played the lead role as Kotter, was a stand-up comedian who talked about the Sweat Hogs in his stage act.

Then ABC came along and offered him a sitcom deal which became Kotter.

John Travolta turned out to become the break out star in the series.

After a couple of weeks at the studio, I got to know a lot about Mr. Travolta.

The first time I met him was in the elevator. He got in on the second floor where his dressing room was.

I was on my way down from the third floor, and I automatically greeted him with the obligatory "Hello."

He looked right at me and did not say one word.

I found that pretty odd since it isn't hard to greet someone when it's one on one in an elevator.

I ran into John again in another elevator on another day, and again he ignored my greeting, and once or twice we passed each other in one of the hallways, and again I was ignored.

I started asking questions about Travolta's manners or lack of them.

I was told by someone who knew him, that since he became a movie star after *Saturday Night Fever* came out, he pretty much changed the way he acted around a lot of people he came into contact with on a daily basis.

The cast of *Welcome Back Kotter* got their scripts for the next show on Fridays. They would rehearse until they filmed the show the next Thursday.

Everyone worked hard and showed up every day except Travolta.

He missed a lot of rehearsal days, and sometimes didn't show up until the real taping day. That lack of commitment pissed a lot of cast members off.

They resented the way he acted and didn't feel that he was any different from anyone else on the show.

During lunch breaks and other time outs from rehearsing, the cast frequently played basketball against the wall of the building across from the cafeteria.

I never saw Travolta playing with his cast members.

The only other one who never played was the man who played Mr. Woodman the Principal on the show.

He was just too old to participate, but he was right there with his fellow actors, leaning on the cafeteria's railing and watching them all play.

One day while the cast was playing basketball, I decided to see if I could find John Travolta.

I went to the second floor of the building where all the dressing rooms were, but no Travolta.

The dressing rooms on that floor were actually small offices which they converted into rooms for the actors.

The actors always complained about their quarters and I couldn't blame them.

I think some of the actors even shared their dressing rooms.

It must have been like trying to live on a submarine.

I continued my search and I walked into a soundstage that I hadn't been in before. It was really neat.

First of all, I was the only one there. If I wanted to, I could yell as loud as I wanted and hear my own echo.

Anyway, the soundstage was decorated for a big party of some sort.

It had a bunch of tables with party hats on them and there was glitter everywhere.

The tables were set for a big event. Plates, glasses, champagne bottles and other stuff. You name it, and it was on the tables.

On the stage was a big sign which spelled out 1977, and then I figured it out that this was a set for a New Year's party.

Only this was October. Not December 31st.

It was for *Dick Clark's Rockin' New Year's Eve Party.*

As it turned out, they would fill up the tables with extras and have a band on stage having a party for New Year's Eve, and everything that they would film would be inserted into the real December 31st show with Dick Clark.

It was a pretty slick operation. Somehow, I felt that I had to keep this party a secret as I continued my search for the missing John Travolta.

§

I looked everywhere for John, but he was nowhere to be found. I went back to my office and continued to work on my own show.

Neil Simon's brother was the Producer of the show. His name was Danny Simon.

In a book that Neil Simon wrote, he gave his brother credit for teaching him how to write.

Personally, I didn't get it, because every joke that Danny would tell was an old joke. I never hear him say or write something that was new and original.

Conversely, whenever I told him about an idea that I had for a sketch, he would tell me that my idea was based on some old joke that had been around for a while.

Danny Simon was in a grumpy mood a lot of the time.

I knew that he had a problem when he bought his niece a new Mercedes for her birthday, and Neil Simon was not happy about that and they started to argue in front of everybody.

The funniest thing I ever saw Danny Simon involved in was when his co-producer brought in a working sketch that he had written and Danny didn't like it.

They argued for a while as the co-producer fought for his work and then he called Danny crazy.

Hearing that, Danny stood up and said, "Who's Crazy? I'm gonna kill you."

And with that, Danny chased his co-producer down the hall past all the offices until they were completely out of sight.

I never heard how all that ended as life at the studio just went on.

I also never did find out where John Travolta was. Even though I took time-out from my writing to look for him

I never even found out where his dressing room was.

I'm sure that other writers and producers came looking for me and found my own office empty, but I was too busy on my personal quest to worry about it.

Travolta must have been on another floor, but I never found him.

I know that his cast members on the show didn't think much of him for bailing out on them.

They felt that if their dressing rooms were good enough for them, then they should be good enough for John Travolta, but obviously, there were not.

He was a big shot. At least, that's what he thought in his own mind.

I even heard that he had an English secretary, but I didn't believe it. It was a bit over the top even for him.

I heard a lot of other things about him, but you can't believe all that stuff.

That's what the celebrity magazines feed on. They make up a lot of stuff that is not true, and then they go ahead and print it.

I once got a call from the National Enquirer, wanting to know information about Farrah Faucet Majors. She was one of the major stars of the television series *Charlie's Angels*.

I wouldn't tell them anything, mainly because I had nothing to say.

Apparently, someone gave them my number and told them that I had some information about the lovely starlet's life. I guess that they got tired of calling me and eventually they left me alone.

On occasion, I would have visitors come into my office. I guess I wasn't the only one who roamed the halls of the studio offices.

Sometimes, there were just writers like me just taking a break from working.

You see when a writer writes, he sometimes hits a brick wall so to speak. He gets stuck on whatever he's writing and he just needs to take a time out to clear his head.

On any sitcom of those days, and even today, you are constantly building up to a great joke, but sometimes you don't know the exact best way to write it.

And so, if you haven't figured it out yet, you take a walk or just goof off and then, when you return to your desk, you have the problem solved and you can come up with that great punch line that you needed.

Sometimes, an actor from Travolta's show would wander into my office and plop down on my great couch.

My desk faced that couch which was a good way for me to have a meeting.

Usually, you'd be sitting in an uncomfortable chair to meet with someone, but not in my office.

Anyway, the actors usually had the same complaint. They're always rehearsing the show using Travolta's stand-in instead of working with the man himself.

He just pulled a lot of no-shows.

And sometimes he wouldn't rehearse at all, and just show up on recording days.

So naturally, his timing was off when they filmed, and he frequently blew his lines.

But because the character he played was kind of slow and stupid, it worked out great.

And when he didn't know his next line, he'd just say, "What? Who? Or Huh," and this actually ended up working for his character because it fit his style.

The problem was that it wasn't written up in the script that way, and he would throw the other actors off.

Many times, they had to stop shooting production and tell John Travolta what his lines were so he could get back into the ebb and flow of the show.

The live studio audience loved it because it was very entertaining, as it just added to the fun of watching a T V show being filmed and getting to see all of your favorite actors doing their thing right in front of you.

This was especially true for the girls in the audience as they always had a favorite "Sweathog" that they adored.

Then, the fateful day arrived. John Travolta appeared at my office door and without a word, sat down.

When I said, "Come in," he already was.

And, from the moment he had entered, his head just moved around like a bobble-head doll.

I tried talking with him, but his answers didn't make any sense.

I didn't know what he was doing in my office if he didn't plan on having a real conversation. He just rambled on in an idiotic fashion.

Then, he got up, but he didn't leave. He disappeared and went into my adjoining office for a few minutes.

I called after him, but he didn't answer.

I got up to see what he was up to, but he reappeared into my office, and without saying a word or shaking my hand, he just left.

No "hello" when he came in and no "good-bye," when he left.

Needless to say, I was dumbfounded.

What the hell was he doing in my office and why was he checking out everything.

Obviously, he had some motive, but what?

I had a lot of work to do, so I couldn't dwell on John Travolta and the weird visit I just had.

I worked late that day and had to finish up a sketch that I was working on.

I had heard earlier from Danny Simon that everything had to be turned in by noon tomorrow the following day.

And, as if I did not have enough to do, I was given sketches from some of the other writers on the same show that needed a few touchups on some of the lines.

So, I had plenty to get done and I was working on a short deadline of noon the next day.

But this was all normal for this show, and I was going to make sure that everything got finished on time.

I went into the cafeteria to grab something to eat and hurried back to my office to jump back into my work load.

When I finally sat down behind my desk, I noticed an envelope addressed to me.

It did not come in the mail. It just had my name on it.

I hurriedly opened it up and began to read. I was totally shocked at its' contents.

That letter came to me from one of the big shots that ran the ABC lot.

I was told to vacate my offices by the following day because someone was taking over my offices.

Needless to say, I was pissed. How dare they.

I picked up my phone to call the people who were in charge of moving people from one office to another, but then I realized that it was too late and everyone had already gone home for the night.

So, I figured that since I had so much work to get done, I'll just show up early the next morning and get my stuff together and find a vacant office or a quiet spot in the cafeteria so that I could get my work finished.

I had a deadline, and I wasn't going to miss it. I couldn't let my producers down. They were all counting on me.

Besides my next job might depend on it because if I do a really good job on this show, there are ·plenty of people who might hire me for another show down the line.

And that was what I always depended on. Word of mouth was my best advertisement when looking for writing work.

I couldn't wait for my agent to call me with another job. She's usually too busy to worry about me. I was probably the last one on her list of calls to make.

I got this job in the first place because Danny Simon happened upon my episode of *All in the Family.*

He loved my script for that show and hired me on the basis of that one screenplay.

Anyway, I went home late that night and even took some of the work with me to stay ahead of the game.

I just had tons of writing to get done and I had to stay ahead of everything in case one of the other writers gave me some more work that had to be completed in a hurry. I had to be prepared for anything that came my way.

The following morning I showed up for work ready and eager to go.

I still hadn't finished my work-load but I was coming in early to get all my stuff done.

I walked into my office and found that all my possessions had been taken off my desk and put onto the floor against the wall.

Also my huge IBM Selectric typewriter was there on the floor and it was on a tilted angle and looked ready to fall over.

My usually neat desk was completely messed up with someone else's stuff, and there was John Travolta's secretary in my middle office.

She instantly upon seeing me, let me know that I was out of these offices and Mr. Travolta was in.

It was obvious to me when I saw models of his jet planes on her new desk.

I didn't have time to cry or even protest about my new predicament, because I was under a fast-approaching deadline to get my work done and handed in.

I would not have been so uncomfortable about the work if I did not have to worry about finding another office to work my miracles in.

I loved my old office. Where else was there a television set that would show other shows being rehearsed anywhere in the entire building? I would miss that diversion.

At my old office I could goof off in style and invite other writer to watch the television with me.

And now, that was all gone and I had to find another way to do my job and still goof off if possible.

Maybe John Travolta will invite me into his new office to watch the actors rehearsing his show. Ha ha!

GILLIGAN'S ISLAND: SHERWOOD SCHWARTZ, BOB DENVER, JIM BACKUS, RUSSEL JOHNSON, AND ALAN HALE JR.

Gilligan's Island is an American sit-com created and produced by Sherwood Schwartz.

The show had an ensemble cast that featured Bob Denver as first mate Gilligan, Alan Hale Jr. as the skipper, and Jim Backus as Thurston Howell the third.

It aired for three seasons on the CBS network (September 26, 1964–April 7, 1967).

It was originally sponsored by Phillip Morris Company and Proctor and Gamble.

The show followed the comic adventures of seven castaways as they attempted to survive the island on which they had been ship-wrecked.

The show immediately enjoyed solid ratings during its original run, and grew in popularity as the crew continued their unsuccessful attempts to escape the island.

Gilligan's Island ran for a total of 98 episodes.

§

SHERWOOD SCHWARTZ CREATER
Sherwood was an American television producer.

He worked on radio shows in the 1940's and created two famous television series called *Gilligan's Island* and *The Brady Bunch*.

BOB DENVER
Bob was an American comedic actor who portrayed Gilligan in the television series from (1964–1967).

JIM BACKUS
Jim was a film and television actor known for his role as Thurston Howell the third in *Gilligan's Island*.

He also was the famous voice of cartoon character, *Mr. Magoo*.

ALAN HALE JR.
Alan played the skipper in *Gilligan's Island*. He also owned a world-famous restaurant in Los Angeles called *The Lobster Barrel*.

He went to school with Mickey Rooney who helped Alan with his career.

Alan booked cruises between shooting episodes of *Gilligan's Island*.

He resembled his father so much that when people saw old movies, they thought it was the Skipper of the Minnow. I guess it was like father, like son.

Alan Hale Jr. borrowed some of his character from the great Oliver Hardy of Laurel and Hardy fame.

§

It seems that the whole world knows of this silly television show.

And if you think about it, you'll probably conjure up something that's stuck in your mind about the show.

It could be the skipper hitting Gilligan with his hat, or Gilligan being chased by wild animals.

Or maybe Ginger, trying to seduce Gilligan for the good of all the castaways.

Gilligan's island will forever be in our collective memories. It's being translated into just about every language imaginable, and some people even believe that these seven, stranded people, are really stuck on an uncharted island.

As the pilot for Gilligan's Island was being shot in Hawaii, the news arrived that President Kennedy had been assassinated.

Everyone was horrified.

The production was completely shut down for several days as no one could believe the horrible news.

Men and women cried.

How could this happen we all thought. How will we ever get through such a tragedy?

But we did, and Gilligan hit the airwaves.

Originally, I had met the creator of *Gilligan's Island* in a small office at Raleigh Studios across the street from the larger Paramount Studio lot.

It was a small office, but Sherwood Schwartz was not a very showy person.

After all, a true writer only needs a pad of paper, a pen and a place to sit. Everything else is bullshit.

At that time, Sherwood was working on a new television show along with his son Lloyd.

Lloyd was a very likable kid, but Sherwood was an unbelievable person.

He was more like your family's favorite uncle or like a friendly mentor who was there to guide you along with whatever project you were working on.

Anyway, he told my partner and me, about a new show that he was planning on doing, and asked if we could come up with some original ideas to throw into the ring with some of the scenes he had already come up with.

Fortunately, in the days that followed, we came up with a few ideas that dazzled Sherwood and he accepted one of them.

At this next meeting, we laid out our ideas and he added his own plots and structure to the discussion and we left with copious notes and some ideas of where to go with the plot.

When our re-write, and the re-write of our re-write was finally over, we had ourselves a job.

All we had to do now, was to come back within a week's time, with a completed script, and our futures in the business were assured.

We turned in our script the following week, and made an appointment to return in a couple of days.

Believe me, those were two of the longest days of our lives as we didn't know what to expect.

Time went by very slowly, and finally· we met with Sherwood's son Lloyd, who simply stared at the two of us when we first sat down, for the longest time without any expression on his face.

And then he spoke. "My father has never done this before and I can't believe that he is doing this now."

Oh, my god, I thought. They hate our stuff and our careers are in the slammer.

Then Lloyd Schwartz continued. "My father," he said, "has never written anything like this on anyone's script before and he has-read hundreds of them.

Lloyd tossed the script to us. On the cover of our script, in large and red printing, it said those most immortal of words:

This is the funniest script I've ever read. Do not change one word of it.

My God. We made it.

Sherwood loved our script. What's next, we both wondered.

Suddenly, and right in front of us, Lloyd let 'the other shoe drop.

Lloyd began to ruffle through our script and then threw it back to us.

"O.K., dad loves it and that's fine with me. Now make it funnier."

But your dad said not to change one word, we protested.

"That's right, but please remember that I am the producer here, and I want you to take it back and work on it. Make it funnier yet.

We were dumb-founded, but we took the script back and of course we made it funnier if that was possible.

Shooting day finally arrived, and we were all excited.

We watched one scene after another being shot at the main studio's largest set.

Then we noticed the character that was playing a Sergeant on the police force was not right.

After that scene was finished, I had some thoughts to share with Sherwood who was there personally directing everything.

I told him that I thought the scene with the policeman was great, but that I had noticed that he did not have a firearm of any type with him.

"You're absolutely right," he said.

"So are you going to shoot it over?" I asked.

"Nope. No one will ever notice. It's fine just the way it is." And he was right. I don't think anyone ever noticed.

Sherwood Schwartz was a genius, wasn't he?

§

A number of years later, I was contacted by Metromedia Television.

They were going to produce a tribute to *Gilligan's Island*, and they wanted me to head up the production.

I wasn't sure how they found me until I met the lead producer whose name was Marion.

Marion was a very tiny woman, but she sure had a lot to say, and she always got directly to the point of any conversation that she was in.

You see, after this idea was approved, someone mentioned my name to her because they knew that I was Sherwood Schwartz's lead writer on the show, and they thought I would know where everyone went to after the final show production was completed.

Now the new idea for this show was basically a marathon of Gilligan Island shows with a character from that specific show talking about the show between commercials.

Unfortunately, Metromedia Television had only set aside enough money to pay for one character to talk about all the various shows and that is where I came into the mix.

Marion was hoping that I would use my relationship with Sherwood Schwartz and maybe get him or another one of the actors to contribute something.

And as it eventually worked out, they got more than they had bargained for.

I looked at this as a way for me to pay back Sherwood for giving me my first big chance to get into the world of television writing.

When I told Sherwood about the proposed project, he loved it and instantly lit up.

He said that he would try to use this great opportunity and reunite the entire cast or as much of the cast as possible.

He just was looking for any excuse to have a few days with everyone. He would pay all the bills.

I reported to Marion that Sherwood would pay for everyone's expenses to come to the shooting location on one day and work the production.

I told her that Sherwood would cover any other expenses if any came up.

Unfortunately, Jim Backus was ill and couldn't attend and Bob Denver was locked into a big project in Chicago and could not get away.

However, there was a local entertainment show in Chicago that would film Bob Denver talking about *Gilligan's Island* for our show. That was so cool.

Tina Louise, who played the beautiful Ginger, just was not invited. I was told that she would make the set an uncomfortable place, and here is why.

Shortly after *Gilligan's Island* began its successful run on television, Tina Louise came into Sherwood's office and told him that she wanted to quit the show.

Sherwood of course was puzzled and asked why. "I was lied to," she replied.

This is Hollywood, my dear. Everyone lies in Hollywood.

"You don't understand Sherwood. I was told that the show was about an actress, played by myself, who is stranded on an island with six other people."

"Well, that is correct," Sherwood replied.

"And he continued by saying that the star of the show was not the actress. It was the skipper and his first mate and that's the way he had set it up and that's the way it has always been."

"And, I certainly never lied to you," he said. "You had the advance scripts in your hand all the time. Everything was always right there for you to see."

Tina stormed out of his office and she let all of the others know how unhappy she was, so when we did our reunion marathon, the unhappy Tina Louise was not asked to attend.

§

I was really jazzed. Since Sherwood was paying for all the actors to attend, my job became easy.

I tried to get an interview from everyone and an immediate problem popped up.

It was in the form of a message on my answering machine.

It said: "Hi Ron. This is the Professor, Russell Johnson. I have to talk with you."

Well, how cool was that?

One of the main actors was actually contacting me and leaving me his telephone number.

I had originally planned to call him back later on and set up a meeting, but there seemed to be something on his mind.

When I called Russel Johnson back, he informed me that while he did not mind doing the show for free, he thought that doing acting or talking about acting for free, might cause him problems with the Screen Actors Guild that they all had to belong to.

He said that his agent was looking into the problem, and it turned out that Russell was right.

They all had to be paid the SAG minimums for the day, and as it turned out, Sherwood Schwartz opened up his check book once again and came to the rescue and paid everyone for one day's work.

Quite a guy Sherwood!

For you see, nothing was going to stop Sherwood from having a nice day for himself and the rest of his old cast from *Gilligan's Island*.

I met up with Russell Johnson a few days later at a restaurant called "The Tail of the Cock." It was located in Studio City, California.

I recalled seeing that restaurant my whole life. During Christmas time, they would decorate the roof with snow and a real sled.

They even had steps leading to the roof where Santa himself met with the children to listen to their wishes. It was a magical time in the valley.

Santa's reindeer were also on the roof which made it an extra special place.

Even Rudolph's nose lit up.

Anyway, I met Russell in the bar area of the restaurant. I ordered and we sat down in a private booth.

I took out my notepad, and he took out a cigarette. I could not believe my eyes. The Professor Smoking.

"I can't believe you're smoking," I said. "The show's Professor Doesn't Smoke. You of all people know how bad cigarettes are for you. You're the Professor."

What I was saying did not seem to bother him. I guess that he gets it all the time.

Anyway, we had a great meeting, and we got a lot of work done.

He told me some of his favorite moments on the show, and I would make sure that we matched his comments to the correct episode.

§

My having lunch with the skipper was another thing.

We met at one of the most famous spots in Hollywood. It is called Musseo and Frank's Restaurant.

It's located on Hollywood Blvd., right near the world-famous Hollywood and Vine cross-streets.

And as the story on Musseo and Frank's Restaurant goes, it seems that all the waiters are part owners or their fathers were before them.

Anyway, it is quite a place It is like going back in time.

This is where all the big Hollywood stars used to hang their hats.

Even most of the stars of today go there.

This restaurant just seems to go on and on.

I arrived with my producer, Marion.

She and I ordered a drink as Alan Hale Jr. entered. He was wearing a big straw hat and a Hawaiian shirt. It was the loudest shirt that I had ever seen.

The first thing he did as he sat down, was to complain about all of the "freaks" walking around in Hollywood these days.

Well, he just seemed to fit in, style wise, and I told him so with a big smile on my face

He thought that was funny, and he gave this great big belly laugh.

The only problem with his belly-laugh, was his arms.

Alan would fling them in either direction when he laughed, and he almost killed Marion where she sat. He really did clonk her.

After the second laugh, she moved much closer to me.

I had never seen anyone laugh like that before. It was truly a sight to behold.

You couldn't just tell anyone about it. They'd just have to see it to believe it.

The only person who looked out of place that day, was Alan. Every-one in the restaurant knew that he was there.

He was just that type of guy. His presence really did fill the entire room.

And he was probably one of the nicest people in that room. Only, just don't sit too close to him.

As we looked at the menus Alan chimed in. "You know I used to have a restaurant in Hollywood."

I answered back. "I know. It was called Alan Hale's Lobster Barrel."

"Did you have a good time there?" he asked.

"Well, let me put it to you this way, Alan. My wife Teri and I ordered two whole lobster dinners. And, what we got were two full grown huge lobsters on our plates. I mean these guys were alive five minutes ago, and now they were on our plates. What were we supposed to do with them? How were we going to eat them? Someone neglected to crack them open and we had a terrible time trying to get at them. Someone in the kitchen should have cracked them apart or something, don't you think?"

Alan's thoughts were all over his face.

Suddenly he began to laugh once more. Marion jumped away from him and practically landed on my lap as his arms were once again on the move.

"I guess that's why my restaurant didn't ever make it. I guess I just didn't know what the hell I was doing."

Alan laughed again and we all laughed with him. "Well," he said, "live and learn."

We continued on with our meeting through the night. Alan was very interesting and a great deal of fun.

Alan would continue to eat and tell stories of old time Hollywood and all the big movie stars he had met over the many years he had been around the studios.

And it was really amazing hearing some of the comments that he made as we all watched his Hollywood weirdos march past our window that faced Hollywood Blvd.

§

I wasn't able to contact some of the other original cast members who were not going to be able to make it.

I would have to have someone else in the cast talk about their role in a specific episode.

Bob Denver was the exception. I was able to contact him by telephone in Chicago.

He had some good stories from the show and treated me very well.

He was truly sorry that he couldn't spend the day that we were going to shoot a few scenes with the other cast members.

§

Instead of using an indoor sound-stage at the studio, we decided to do the shoot at Marina Del Rey.

Marina Del Rey is a very up-scale and very fancy docking location for most of the better yachts in the area.

It is located just north of the Los Angeles Inter-National Airport.

My oldest son Stuart was ten years old, and he had a special place in his heart for yachts and he joined us on the day of the big shoot.

Alan Hale Jr. was going to be our first shot of the day.

Alan was seated on a boat which was supposed to be a stand-in for the real ship from the series.

When the director yelled the word, "ACTION," everyone heard a loud splash.

We all looked around as Alan Hale Jr. jumped up and ran towards the sound.

My son, Stuart, had accidently fallen into the Marina waters.

Alan was there in a flash and safely pulled him from the water.

And to this day, my son boasts that he was the only person in the entire world, who was rescued by the Skipper from *Gilligan's Island*.

GROWING UP IN ENCINO, CALIFORNIA, STEVE ALLEN

Steve Allen was born December 26, 1921, and he died at the age of 78 in Los Angeles on October 20, 2000.

He died of a 'heart attack that he suffered when he was in an auto accident.

His entire name was Stephen Valentine Patrick William Allen.

He was an American television personality, musician, composer, actor, comedian and writer.

Though he got his start in radio, he is best known for his television career.

He first gained national attention as a guest host on the very popular Arthur Godfrey talent show.

He left there to become the first host of the tonight show where he was instrumental in innovating the concept of the television talk show.

Thereafter, he hosted numerous game and variety shows, including the Steve Allen show, and the I've got a secret show.

He was a regular panel member of the CBS's show, *What's my Line*.

Allen was a great pianist, and a prolific composer, having written over 14,000 songs.

He won the 1964 gammy awards for best original jazz composer.

He wrote 56 books and has two stars on the Hollywood walk of fame.

His home town was Chicago, Illinois.

§

Encino, California is one of the wealthiest places in the world alongside Beverly Hills.

One is in the city, and the other is in the valley.

Encino became rich beginning in the 1980's when it suddenly became a most desirable place to live.

The musical group, The Jackson Five had a big piece of property which once housed a small zoo.

It is right off of Ventura Boulevard in the very heart of Encino.

People still crowd around in front of the front gate hoping to get a glimpse of one of the Jackson's.

Edgar rice Burroughs, the creator of Tarzan also lived right off Ventura Boulevard, as did Bud Abbott and Lou Costello who were just down the road a bit.

Even the great Clark Gable was a stone's throw away from Ventura Boulevard. (Of course, now, it is known as the Clark Gable Estates.)

Also, Liberace's house was nearby and also off of Ventura Boulevard.

When I was just a kid growing up in Encino, that just happened to be where you lived. It was really considered a rich area then.

At that time, the whole of the San Fernando Valley was just beginning to be developed.

If your family took you out for a fancy dinner, you might be able to catch a glimpse of actor John Wayne or some other famous star.

If you lived in the Valley, you really never knew who you might see shopping at the same grocery store that you were in at any time of the day.

I remember seeing a couple of movie stars one Halloween night while out trick or treating.

As the sun went down, and the moon came up, we always left our houses all dressed up in our Halloween costumes carrying empty treat bags.

We were determined to fill them up.

This was a time when a candy bar cost a nickel and that was considered expensive.

Royal Oak Road was technically in the adjoining city to where I would always go trick and treating which was in Encino, but Encino and Tarzana were so close to each other that the perception of where one was walking was always kind of blurred, not that it mattered.

The homes here were absolutely gorgeous, and the streets were really wide.

This made it the perfect street for all of us to go trick or treating.

It was also the route we walked on our way to the bus stop, so we knew it well.

One of the first homes was really familiar to us. It seemed that every time we walked by as a group of two or more, someone would come out of that house and scold us for talking too loud.

Apparently, an older silent film star lived there and was not in good health.

But if you tell a kid on Halloween that you could not make as much noise as you wanted, then they would do exactly what they wanted to do anyway.

We were just kids and what did we know? But we did scream like ghouls out of pure fun anyway.

After the silent house, we came to a house on a hill. It was quite the hike up, but it was well worth it.

It was probably the only house for miles around that gave out treats.

Would you believe that instead of candy, they would give each of us who were in costume, a real silver dollar. Wow.

We were all dumbfounded at our good fortune.

Those sweet people commented about what we were wearing and then the money began to flow.

Now it wasn't that we were bad kids, but I guess there is a streak of greediness in all of us.

By the time we got back to the street, there was more than one of us who thought the same thing.

If we went home and changed into a different Halloween Costume, then we could go back to that same house and get another silver dollar.

And after a few comments to each other, we broke up our discussion and all ran back to our own house to try and come back with something new in the way of a costume. A silver dollar was a lot of money and we all wanted more.

Screw the candy. We all knew that it was the silver dollars we wanted and we were going to get them.

§

Later after getting our ill-gotten-gains, we moved on to new hunting grounds.

If a house looked empty of candy givers, our trick or treaters would move onto what looked like a friendlier place.

The house on the left had a lot of stairs leading up to the front door, but we had heard that an old-time movie star lived there and we wanted to see what she was giving out.

There were rumors that she drank a lot of alcohol, but we'd give her the benefit of the doubt and call upon her.

Up the steps we all went and rang the bell. A few minutes passed and we could sense that someone was on the other side of the closed door.

This house belonged to famous movie star, Gale Storm. She had a big name and reputation in Hollywood and now we were there at her door.

Finally, the door opened and a house servant passed out candy to fill our hungry bags.

I took a step back and noticed that behind the servant and

watching all of us, was Hollywood Star, Gale Storm.

She had a drink in one hand and some autographed pictures in the other.

I asked her for her autograph, and she gave me a picture of herself.

When she did, she kissed me on the cheek. I could smell the liquor on her. It had the same awful smell as it did on my own father.

I never liked that smell, but I was happy to meet her and we moved on to the house next door that also belonged to a very famous person.

Steve Allen was one of the great comedians of his time. He was like a Jerry Seinfeld in his day.

When he was on stage, he would talk about a lot of things that he had observed as he wandered around the "street of Los Angeles."

At this time, he was the new host of *The Tonight Show*.

He had put his personal touch to the late-night show and had made it his own show-place.

One of the funniest signature events that he had on his show, was his running bit called "The Man on the Street." This was a very popular event and everyone looked forward to it.

Steve Allen was very popular and was highly respected in show business for many, many years.

His house was on the next corner where I remembered one day after school when our bus dropped us off across from his house.

They were filming something pretty cool outside on his front lawn. There were a bunch of guys made up to look like real Indians.

They wore war-paint and carried real knives, bows and arrows. This had to do with a sketch about the Indians wanting to take back Steve Allen's house.

They claimed that it belonged to them and they demanded that Steve move out or they would be going to war.

Well, you guessed it. Steve Allen refused their demands and the arrows began to fly all around.

Our group of watching schoolkids had to stay back and away from where-ever the action was going on, but we got to see everything.

It was very exciting to watch and it was all being caught on film so Steve could show it on his program.

We were watching the Indians creeping up the small hill that surrounded his house, and just as they got to the top of the hill, they were met with lots of resistance from Steve and the good guys that he had with him.

Ultimately, the big battle for Steve's house was won by the Steve Allen group, and it was a pretty cool sight to behold, especially for a bunch of elementary school kids just coming off their school bus.

And so on Halloween night, Steve Allen's house seemed like a pretty good stop for my group of dressed up ghouls who were out to get some candy.

We all agreed that Steve Allen was a nice guy and whenever any of us saw his late-night show, Steve and his many guests were always interesting.

There was no gate surrounding Steve's house so it was really easy to just walk up to his door and ring the bell.

We heard someone playing the piano inside, but after we rang the bell the piano went silent.

Then the door opened and we all yelled, "Trick or Treat."

To our surprise and happiness, we locked all our eyes on Steve Allen.

He was the only one who did not have someone else answering the door for him. He answered it himself and we were all delighted.

And as a further surprise, he invited all of us into his home. He beckoned for us to follow him in, which we did.

After a few moments, we found ourselves at Mr. Allen's piano.

He sat down and was getting ready to play for us but he first explained the deal.

Steve was going to play the piano for us.

When he finished, and if we clapped wildly for him, then we would get to reach into this huge bowl of candy and take whatever it was that we could grab.

If we didn't clap, our punishment was that we did not get any candy and we would have to sit there and listen to him play another song.

That was how it worked.

If you were a music lover, you were in piano heaven. If you just wanted the candy, you needed to get with the program.

And as we finally left with our candy rewards, we clued in the next group of kids who followed our group, about listening to Steve Allen play the piano and then get some of the great candy.

Steve Allen had it all figured out for the kids. He was a great guy and we all loved him.

After Halloween, I tried watching the Steve Allen television show whenever I could.

I am sure that I became his biggest fan—ever.

For some reason, I felt comfortable watching his show. I always thought that if I ever knocked again at his door, that he would welcome me in and play the piano for me.

I also did wonder if that large bowl of candy was always atop the piano, or was it just there for the neighborhood kids on Halloween who came around to listen and clap for him.

I'll always remember Mr. Steve Allen. He earned the right to have all of America clapping for him, personally and privately.

For me, he was just an all-around great guy.

HANNA BARBERA PRODUCTIONS,
THE THREE STOOGES

After a very successful number of years at MGM studios, Bill Hanna and Joe Barbera opened their own studio and single-handedly invented the television cartoon shows for kids on Saturday mornings.

Throughout their many years at the studio's, Hanna and Barbera collected seven Oscars, eight Emmy's and their own star on the Hollywood walk of fame.

Creating more than one thousand cartoon characters, Hanna and Barbera productions dominated the cartoon field for years and years.

By the mid 1980's the company's fortunes declined somewhat after the profitability of Saturday morning cartoons was eclipsed by weekly afternoon syndication.

The company was eventually purchased by ted turner, mainly for its catalog of film and cartoons that he wanted.

Ted Turner's Turner Broadcasting company was purchased by Time Warner and Hanna Barbera closed their doors shortly thereafter.

William Hanna died in 2001 and his studio rights became a subsidiary called Warner Brothers animation in name but, in reality, was dissolved.

Currently Hanna-Barbera is just a popular name slapped onto

productions of old studio classic works.

Hanna-Barbera was always based in Universal City, California.

§

THE THREE STOOGES

Three funny guys called themselves *The Three Stooges*.

They were Moe Howard, Curly Howard and Larry Fine.

They were an American vaudeville and comedy act of the early mid-20th century, best known for their numerous short films by Columbus studios which are still being shown on kids shows in today's television markets.

Their trademark was physical farce and slapstick.

In their films, the three stooges were always known as Moe, Larry and Curly.

The act became famous in vaudeville of the 1920's and were billed under the cover name of Ted Healy and his three stooges.

Their everlasting fame was guaranteed when Hanna Barbera studios bought the rights to make their likenesses into cartoons to be shown on kids shows.

§

HANNA-BARBERA, JOE RUBY, AND KEN SPEARS

Joe and Ken were animation writers at Hanna Barbera studios.

They created a lot of shows for the powerhouse animation company, bur their- biggest hit was in 1968 when they created a show about a bunch of kids driving around in a van with their cowardly dog that they thought was so brave.

Scooby Doo was a tremendous hit for the studio.

In the beginning, the boys wrote most of the episodes so they could control what they wanted the show to do and the direction they wanted it to head.

This was fine with the bosses.

Then it was back to creating other shows while *Scooby Doo* was placed in the hands of others.

ABC in their infinite wisdom, decided to use the powerhouse of Ruby/Spears to compete against their own Hanna Barbera, and they rented a building down the street near the iconic Hollywood Bowl.

Their thinking was that Ruby-Spears Productions, also owned by ABC, would take some of the work load off of the super busy Hanna-Barbera company.

They moved the *Scooby Doo* staff and new writers over to the new building.

At the same time as all the moving around was going on, the rights for the comedy trio, *The Three Stooges*, were up for grabs.

The studio thought that if they owned the rights, they could use them to turn out cartoons which should be tremendous sellers since everyone loved *The Three Stooges*.

So in order to secure the rights, they had to find out who owned them. And right there in Hollywood, right under their noses, so to speak, was a man named Norman Mauer.

Mr. Mauer was married to Moe Howard's daughter.

It turned out that Moe Howard, one of the original of *The Three Stooges*, was the smartest Stooge of them all.

He had fought for and gained all rights to the ownership of the name and use of the characters, and when he died he left all these rights to his daughter.

So all the studio basically had to do was to employ the daughter's husband, and when he took the job that they would offer him, it was under a specific condition that they could purchase the rights to the Stooges.

It sounds nice and simple. Give the man a job at the studio and in return have him sell off his family story rights. Sounded nice and simple but.it did not turn out that way.

Mr. Mauer agreed to make a deal with the studio if he could have the position of producer for one of the episodes and that his son came along with the deal and would be a mini boss.

The deal was done and the studio now had all rights to the

three stooges and my fellow writers and I were all excited to meet with our new mini-boss for the first script but we never did see him, meet with him, get any thoughts or ideas from him.

In other words, his door was closed to us and he never would look at the work we were doing.

His door was always closed and locked from the inside. We could hear him talking on the telephone but he would not open his door to us, so we would take turns listening to his end of the many telephone calls that he was making trying to find himself another job to go to when this one would end shortly.

To our collective knowledge, he never got another job in the industry, but we could be wrong. After the first cartoon script was turned into a regular cartoon we found his office empty and the person who occupied it long gone.

The offices of ruby/spears of which I was a part, was a hub of activity.

It was during the 1980's, when video games were all the rage.

And every time a new game came out, someone from the top of our organization would decide to try and make a cartoon out of it. We were kept very busy and loving it.

Different companies brought their video machines into our offices for us to play with1 and that was exactly what we did.

We didn't work. We played. It was strictly research of course.

Too bad we weren't in Silicon Valley at the time working with their computers.

ABBOTT AND COSTELLO

William "Bud" Abbott and Lou Costello were an American comedy duo whose work in Vaudeville and on stage, radio, film and television, made them the most popular comedy team during the 1940's and 1950's.

Their patter (talk) routine of "Who's on First?" Is one of the best-known comedy routines of all time and set the framework for many of their best-known comedy bits.

Bud Abbott (1897 - 1974) was a veteran burlesque entertainer from a show business family.

Lou Costello (1906 -1959) had been a burlesque comic since 1930.

Universal studios signed them to a long-term contract and they did so well at the box office that they actually saved the studio from going out of business.

Bud and Lou made 36 films together between 1940 and 1956.

They were among the most popular and highest paid entertainers in the world earning on average of $789,000 each year per person.

In 1941, Abbott and Costello had their prints set in concrete at what was then known as "Grauman's Chinese Theatre."

In 1942 they were the absolute top box office draw with four films.

"Who's on First?" Is their signature routine, and it made the world laugh.

Abbott and Costello did many voice overs for many cartoon characters for Hanna and Barbera studios.

Abbot and Costello are the only non-baseball players inducted into the Baseball Hall of Fame with their famous routine leading the way.

BUD ABBOTT

William "Bud" Abbott and Lou Costello were an American comedy team duo, whose work in vaudeville and on stage, screen, radio, film and television, made them the most popular comedy team during the 1940's and 1950's.

Their routine "Who's on First?" is considered to be one of the greatest comedy routines of all time and it set the framework for many of their other best known comedy hits and bits.

Bud Abbott (1897- 1974) was a veteran burlesque entertainer from a show business family.

When he met his future partner in comedy, Abbott was already performing in "Minsky's Burlesque Shows."

Lou Costello had been a burlesque comic since 1930 after failing to break into movie acting.

He worked as a stunt double and film extra for many years.

Together, they were highly successful as Abbott played the devious straight man and Costello played the stumbling, dim-witted laugh getter.

In 1951, the team moved to television as rotating hosts of the Colgate Comedy Hour.

Eddie Cantor and Martin and Lewis were among the other hosts.

Each show was a live one hour show of vaudeville in front of a live studio audience.

Abbott and Costello were inducted into the New Jersey hall of fame in 2009.

§

Universal Studios was not doing so well in the late 1930's and into the early 1940's.

Then the comedy team of Abbott and Costello pulled Universal's fat out of the fire.

Fate dealt a gracious blow for the studios when in 1939, someone thought that they were hiring a dancing troupe.

Its name was the Bud Abbott dancers.

Yes, that was a legitimate dance company that belonged to someone else.

But instead of hiring this company for a movie called, *One Night in The Tropics*, they hired by mistake Abbott and Costello.

And as they say, the rest was history.

After a brief appearance in this movie, Bud and Lou starred in the block-buster, *Buck Privates*.

This was a new beginning for Universal Pictures. It was also the beginning of 36 movies starring the comedy team who came along at the beginning of World War Two when all of America needed to laugh.

And laugh they did. Bud and Lou also earned around 80 million dollars in war bonds for our country in those very early war years.

§

I met Bud Abbott in 1969. Ten years earlier, Lou Costello had passed away.

My college roommate knew that I was a big fan of the team and as my great luck would have it, he knew the location of Bud Abbott.

It seems that my room-mate's father was the owner of a dry-cleaning shop in the San Fernando Valley and one of his regular customers was Mr. Abbott.

After getting the address, I boldly pulled up to his very small house in Reseda.

On his mailbox, there was one of Bud's sayings: "HI YA NEIGHBOR."

It seems that in Bud's lifetime, he'd met so many people that he couldn't possibly remember all their names, so he always called most people "Neighbor," and that was how it read on his mailbox.

I sat in my car which was parked in front of his house for the longest time.

My 70's stripped down Dodge Challenger finally kicked me out, and I headed to the front door.

I finally got up the nerve and tapped on his door ever so slightly. I was nervous as all hell.

Suddenly, the door slowly opened with a creak. It was just like an old movie he would have played in.

I peered inside and saw Bud Abbott sitting about five feet to my right. He was wearing a bathrobe.

The television was immediately to my left and he was very close to it.

A man in a white coat had opened the door. It was his day nurse.

"Hi Bud, I said. I'm a really big fan of yours, and I'd just like to talk with you, if you don't mind."

That wasn't exactly what I had planned on saying, but after my seeing him like he was, my whole speech went out the window.

Bud waived me in.

"Come in friend." I took one step in and the door closed behind me. The nurse went about his duties and Bud directed me to a chair close to him.

Then there was complete silence as Bud went back to watching television.

I remember that it was a baseball game between the Dodgers and the Giants. It was the only baseball series that was televised in those days.

The year was 1970 and Bud sat in a chair from the 1900's.

Above him was an oil picture of himself which was done while he was in burlesque. It looked elegant. I'd look at the portrait and then at Bud himself.

I'd hate to say that it was a letdown, but it was. Two different people in one place. One person was real and the other was really old.

During a commercial break on the television, I told Bud that my name was Ron, and that I had always been a huge fan of Abbott and Costello.

I could tell that he liked hearing that, and to my great surprise he said, "Yeah, I miss my little buddy."

It had been about ten years since Lou Costello had passed away and I could see that Bud truly missed him.

Now, the game was back on and the room grew silent. Bud only wanted to talk between innings.

When another break came, Bud now called me "Rod," even though I corrected him.

I thought that maybe he didn't hear me but he really did. He was being funny in his own way.

From the other room came a "TROLL" looking figure. She sat in another chair close to Bud.

I was introduced to her as Mrs. Bud Abbott. She definitely had a weight problem.

When she sat, she had to spread her legs so that her stomach could rest on the chair.

Then Bud gave her an order on my behalf. It was really directed at the houseboy.

"Bring Rod some champagne."

Bud's wife chimed in. "Bud," she said. "He's not old enough to drink champagne. "Sure he is," Bud retorted, "C'mon, bring the stuff in. Bring in Rod's drink."

Betty Abbott interrupted, but Bud cut her off, "Shut up, you old bat." When Bud spoke up, he had a kind of gravelly voice.

I was shocked. I couldn't believe what I started.

I didn't know at the time, that Bud called her an old bat all the time. I guess it would be a learning experience for me.

Needless to say, I didn't get any champagne that day. After all I was still 17 years old and I admitted it. Truth is, I didn't like the stuff.

If they offered me a beer or some scotch, I might have lied about my age, but that didn't happen.

I was just happy to be in Bud Abbott's house even though

it wasn't like the mansions that he must have been used to when he was making big money out of Hollywood. It was just a small house off Ventura Blvd. in Reseda.

I made my visit short until the next time I popped in which was about one month later. Only this time I decided to bring a friend along.

I grew up with Gary. He was my best friend and he was as crazy about Abbott and Costello as I was.

I clearly remember when we were little boys and our parents took us to the local grocery store. It was called Bestway Market and it was on Ventura Blvd.

It was right down the street from Bud Abbott's mansion that he had in those days.

On this specific day, we saw Lou Costello in the market. We felt that we had to do something, so when Costello looked in our direction, we yelled: "Hayyyyyyy Abbbbbtttttt.

Costello looked at us and laughed.

Then we knew that we had to get out of there and we ran outside.

Who knew what the store manager might do to us? Anyway, that was my one and only meeting with the famous Lou Costello.

Costello lived about five miles down the street from Abbott. He lived there at the beginning of the city that they called Studio City.

I guess that the city got its name because way back in the early days, the local movie studio was called Republic Pictures.

The studio changed its name over all the years, but while it was Republic Studios, John Wayne filmed hundreds of pictures here.

Anyway, it finally became Studio City, and it's been called that for some time. The "Seinfeld Show" spent nine years on that lot and MTM (Mary Tyler Moore) productions were also filmed there.

That's a very short history of studio city.

Anyway, Costello's house was about one block north of Ventura Blvd. on Longridge Street.

At Christmas time, the police had to be called in to direct traffic there.

This was because the Costello house had great exhibits and lights. Lou even hired a Santa Claus to hand out candy canes to everyone who came by to look at his place.

And, on occasion, Costello would come out and visit with the cars full of people who came to see his house.

Lou Costello would always have a handful of personal pictures which he autographed.

He really loved Christmas and shared himself with everyone.

§

MORE BUD ABBOTT

During one of my trips to Abbott's house, I found out that he had recently had a stroke which had paralyzed half his body.

This was why he never got out of his chair, especially in front of me. I believe that Bud didn't want me to know how bad off he really was.

Whenever I came to visit, I never stayed long. I did not want to wear out my welcome, so my visits were always short.

Bud really seemed to like that and he always made me feel welcome.

In front of Bud's chair was a type of hospital table. On it was his two-inch cigarette holder with a carton of his Pall Mall cigarettes.

Bud loved to smoke and to me he seemed to be a chain smoker who would light up his next cigarette just as he was finishing off the last one.

Everyone in the house smoked, including me. I never noticed if the house man smoked because when I was there, he didn't come around much.

Once when I came over unannounced which I always did, Bud was watching a Dodger Game against the Giants.

When the camera panned the baseball fans, I told Bud that

almost every person at Candlestick Park knew who he was.

Hearing this, he started to cry. He quickly regained his composure and told me that he thought that he had been forgotten by just about everyone.

I assured him that he was all wrong about this, and that he was well loved the world over. I know that made him feel good.

His mind was still sharp, and I knew that there wasn't much that he had forgotten.

He still called me Rod instead of Ron, and I thought that he felt he was just being funny, so I stopped correcting him.

On one occasion his wife Betty again said something to him.

His quick response was the usual "shut up you old bat."

On the surface, it sounded mean, but it really wasn't. That was just their relationship. She laughed and he laughed and in time, I learned to laugh too.

§

My best friend Gary finally got up the guts to come with me on one of my visits. He was apprehensive about coming along, but he relented.

He was so excited to meet his idol, and then in front of Bud Abbott, the two of us proceeded to perform, "Who's on First" for Bud, who seemed to be loving it.

We were doing a great job and having a lot of fun doing it. We could see that Bud was going along with us and was mouthing the words as we did them.

"Who's on First" never sounded so good except, of course when Bud and Lou did it.

Suddenly Gary forgot his line, and Bud threw it in.

IT WAS PERFECT. Gary recovered and we finished the entire routine with a perfect performance.

Bud Abbott even clapped for us and he called for champagne all around to celebrate our performance.

Gary asked Bud Abbott a bunch of dumb questions, and then asked me if we could leave.

I knew that he had his fill and it was time to take him out.

It was interesting since I knew that he personally loved Abbott and Costello, but for some reason he was uncomfortable with just Bud Abbott by himself. Gary never came back with me to visit with Abbott again.

I never could figure out why I kept coming back but I did over and over.

I knew Abbott loved it when I came over, and I loved each and every visit that we had.

Early on, I realized that Abbott didn't like talking about Lou Costello that much. And when I did want to know something about the team, I was made to feel as if I was prying into his personal business and so I stopped asking.

Abbott did like living and talking about the past, and he enjoyed showing pictures of what he used to look like and all the things that he used to own until the Internal Revenue Service took it all away from him.

From what he told me, it never made any sense how he and Lou Costello lost most of their fortunes to the IRS.

It was in the 1940's when Bud and Lou traveled across the United States and Europe raising money for the war effort.

They brought in around 80 million dollars for our government.

For Lou's trouble, he contracted rheumatic fever and never really recovered from it.

So here it was, years later and the boys' who were victims of bad accountants, watched as the government raked them over the coals and took away their hard-earned fortunes.

Can these two, innocent sweet-hearts really be blamed?

What happened to their grateful government for whom they raised millions and millions of dollars to help them win the war?

Where was the hand of justice? Why didn't the President of the United States intervene and tell the IRS to lay off Abbott and Costello?

Somebody should have done something, but nothing was ever done to help them and as it turned out, the hand of justice was around their necks, and never let go.

Of course, this is just my own personal opinion.

It all made no sense. In the end, I think it helped kill them both.

It wasn't as if they didn't have any connections.

They were asked to the White House many times and they performed "Who's on First" in front of several sitting presidents.

I don't think I ever saw Abbott not wearing a bathrobe. I understand this because I never knew him to go out of his house anywhere.

But I did come by on Christmas Eve and Abbott was very excited to see all the Christmas lights that completely surrounded his house.

Betty had paid a service to put lights up around the fence of their home.

Bud told me that he wanted my help so that he could see the lights from the front of his house. I helped him get up and I helped him out onto the front porch.

Abbott used me for his crutch and he was pretty heavy.

Then Abbott spotted some broken glass in the street and noticed that several of his Christmas lights had been stolen.

He suddenly got a lot heavier as he leaned on me. He began to cry. How could people steal from him and especially on Christmas?

I had to leave, but I stayed with Abbott until he felt better.

That meant getting him back into his chair and getting him a glass of champagne with a lit cigarette.

I found an old Abbott and Costello movie with Boris Karloff.

Abbott didn't object to watching one of his movies again.

His eyes stared transfixed on the screen as the movie played. I could see that he was happy again and that made me happy, too.

§

I hadn't seen Abbott for a couple of weeks, but I did see the front page of the National Enquirer. It said, "Bud Abbott Near Death."

Oh my God, I thought. I had to get over to see Abbott.

The next day, I got to Abbott's house. I ran toward the door and knocked loudly. This time Betty answered the door, and I could instantly see Bud, sitting in his chair, and he looked just fine, at least for someone who was 73 years old and was half paralyzed.

I asked Bud about that awful picture in the Enquirer, and he told me that they took the picture when he was in the middle of sneezing.

During the interview by the reporter, Abbott said that he sneezed a couple of times while the photographer took some pictures, but he didn't realize what kind of pictures the man was taking.

Bud got calls from all over the world about the cover of the magazine.

While Bud was definitely a sick man who had many health problems, the picture that they published was pretty awful and very unfair to the readers of the magazine.

I was very happy to see that my friend was okay.

Bud asked me when my friend Jerry was coming back. I reminded Bud that his name was Gary, not Jerry.

But, Bud continued to refer to us as Rod and Jerry. He still liked being a funny guy.

A lot of my friends came with me to visit Bud Abbott. Unfortunately, they always wanted to ask him questions about Lou Costello.

I told them again and again that they should not bring it up unless Abbott does, but they didn't pay attention to what I asked of them, and their visits did not go well.

The fact of the matter was, well, it usually brought Abbott to tears and I had to stop bringing my friends around.

From my many, many visits, I always seemed to know what Abbott enjoyed talking about, and I kept our conversations in his comfort zone.

He liked to talk about what big shots he and Costello were back in the old days.

He liked to talk about their legendary poker games, and how some of the pots were well over ten thousand dollars.

In those days, they had a lot of time to kill on their movie sets, and they used that time playing poker.

Sometimes they would hold up film production, while one of their friends went to the bank to get some more cash.

Abbott always brought up the fact that Costello was not a very good gambler, and it was usually Abbott himself who would wipe him out at the poker games.

Many a director got mad at them for holding up the shooting.

But that was just the way it was.

When you were a star, you could get away with just about anything. Abbott always got a kick out of telling me about all of that.

Abbott's all-time favorite movie from the team of Abbott and Costello, was called, *Hold That Ghost*. It had a snappy script and he enjoyed the fast pace of the movie.

The movie was as funny as could be. Its original title was *The Ghost Steps Out*, but it was later changed.

Bud was in love with many of their movies that allowed them to use some of their old routines from their vaudeville days.

One movie called *The Time of Their Lives* actually split up the comedy team for the first and last time.

Abbott played a modem doctor and Costello played a revolutionary war character from the past.

Lou's ghostly character harassed Bud throughout the movie and Bud really got to show a serious side to his acting.

They all thought that it was a charming movie with a lot of heart but the movie was not a big hit.

Abbott and Costello Meet Frankenstein, was another blockbuster for the studio.

While in the midst of shooting, Costello wanted to use an old routine of theirs from years ago.

Charles Barton, the director butted heads with Costello over this, but Costello insisted and the director finally gave in.

One routine featuring Costello went on and on until Costello finally was exhausted and he yelled at his director, "When are you gonna cut"?

"When you do something funny," was the sarcastic reply.

From that time forward, Costello played actor and Charles Barton did the directing.

The film was a big success and Charles Barton and the team made seven more movies which were all big hits.

I was out of town in college when Bud Abbott passed away.

I heard it on the news programs and many of my friends called me up to offer condolences.

Bud Abbott was a great guy who had a hard and fast life.

He drank a lot and smoked up a storm and I never thought that his body could ever catch up with his great mind.

And in the end, Bud Abbott was my good friend and I think about him a lot.

JOE COCKER

John Robert "Joe" Cocker (may 20,1944–December 22, 2014

Joe Cocker was an English rock, blues and soul singer, and a great musician.

He was known for his gritty voice, spasmodic body movements in his performances, and his cover versions of popular songs, particularly those of the singing group called the Beatles.

Cocker's cover album of the Beatles, "with a little help from my friends." Reached number one in the United Kingdom in 1961.

He performed his song live at Woodstock in 1969 and at the party at the palace concert for the golden jubilee of queen Elizabeth II in the year2002.

His 1974 cover line of "you are so beautiful" reached number 5 in the United States.

Cocker was the receiver of several special awards including 1983's Grammy Award for his United States number one album with Jennifer warner called *Up Where We Belong*.

In 1993, he was nominated for the British award as best British male singer.

He had been ranked 97th on the *Rolling Stone* magazine's 100 greatest singers list.

I always heard that Joe Cocker was a great musician.

"They" said that his voice was one in a million, and when he sang, his arms flailed. about in all directions.

It was said that it was as if he was playing a piano and an air guitar at the same time.

In Los Angeles' San Fernando Valley, there was a big entertainment club that opened in the 1970's.

It was called the "Tennessee Gin & Cotton Club"; and it was massively big.

It had several completely stocked bars running throughout the entire complex, and there were several rooms where performers sang and played their music in semi-quiet areas.

Every visit to the Club was a complete surprise.

You never knew who you might be listening too when you went into a room and sat down with the required drink in your hand.

"We" went into a room that started to rapidly fill up with people and there was a great buzz of excitement and energy inside the area.

I asked around, but no one seemed to know who it was that was going to perform for us. The excitement kept building until the performer finally took the stage.

Joe Cocker came into the room and simply dominated the entire audience with his songs that went on for about an hour.

It was an absolutely amazing performance and we left knowing that we had seen something special playing out in front of us.

I personally went back to the Club several times, but could never connect with someone who had the same star power as Joe Cocker, who had just glued us to our seats from start to finish of his performance.

I guess we were just lucky that special Joe Cocker night. HOW OFTEN DO YOU GET TO HEAR FROM SOMEONE WHO HAD PLAYED AT "WOODSTOCK"?

§

I had begun writing scripts for Norman Lear shows like *Good Times* and *All in The Family*.

And I remember one particular night when I stayed to watch a taping of *All in The Family*.

I stood in the very back of the studio with the producers, when I noticed someone in the audience who was attracting attention.

It appeared that his arms were flailing about in what we all thought was an uncontrollable manner to the music that introduced the show.

We summoned security because we thought he was probably going to cause a disturbance.

I walked down the stairs to see if I could be of any help, and I got a good look at the troublemaker.

To my surprise, it was Joe Cocker, just being himself, as he reacted to the music that he was hearing.

Security was called off, and Joe was given an open area where he could relax and enjoy our show without disturbing anyone.

The taping went on without a hitch, and everyone was happy, especially me, as I watched one of my favorite performers doing his thing as he watched and listened to one of my shows.

Joe Cocker was one talented guy, and I was honored to have him with us that afternoon.

WAYNE NEWTON

Carson Wayne Newton was born April 3, 1942 and is one of the most famous American singers and entertainers.

Wayne Newton is known as Mr. Las Vegas, Mr. Entertainment, and the Midnight Idol.

His best-known songs include 1972's "Daddy Don't You Walk So Fast, 1965's "Red Roses for a Blue Lady" and "Danke Schoen" from 1963.

Many prominent entertainment icons were helpful in his long-lived career.

He either appeared with or made a guest appearance upon a show with Lucille Ball, Bobby Darin, Danny Thomas, George Burns and Jack Benny.

From 1980 through 1982 he performed with the "Beach Boys."

In 2007, Newton revealed on the Larry King live show, that he had a problem with Johnny Carson of *The Tonight Show.*

He said that Johnny Carson made jokes about him and was a mean spirited human being.

There were verbal attacks between these two well-known entertainers for many years.

From 1980 to 1982, Wayne Newton was part owner of the Aladdin hotel.

He was involved in a partnership that led to a number of lawsuits and a failed attempt by Newton to purchase the entire hotel for himself in 1983.

In 1992, Wayne Newton filed for Chapter 11 bankruptcy to reorganize an estimated 20 million dollars in personal debt.

In honor of Wayne Newton's great success in Las Vegas or a lack to bigger names, the airport was referred to as the Wayne Newton Airport for a time.

Dave Barry was a Las Vegas fixture.

He had been around for a very long time as Wayne Newton's opening act.

My partner and I were lucky enough to get the job of writing jokes for Wayne Newton's opening act, and this was by no means an easy gig.

Dave Barry was our boss and taskmaster. It was hard to make up a joke he didn't already know the punch line to.

But try we did. We worked like crazy to please Mr. Barry.

It was kind of a crazy time in the lives of two young writers.

We worked our butts off to try and write original material for our boss and it usually ended up with him already knowing the punch lines.

Looking back at all this, I guess our young minds only thought that we were being original. It didn't matter how much we scoured the newspapers for new and refreshing topics to write about, Dave Barry still knew our punch lines.

Fortunately for us, we prodded along and still, once in a while, managed to write fresh material that Dave didn't have the answer to.

After all, that was our job.

Dave Barry performed two shows a night. He stayed on stage at the Sands Hotel until a red light from the back of the showroom came on.

That meant that it was time for Wayne Newton to start his stage show.

Our hotel room and all expenses were paid for by the Sands Hotel. We thought we had a pretty large room, but Dave Barry's room was just about double our size and was located at the top of the tower floors.

His room was amazingly massive at about two thousand square feet and it came complete with a butler.

Our daily routine was very difficult and full of pressure.

Our day began with writing in our room, and when we thought that we had enough material to impress Mr. Barry, we called ahead to see if we could meet with him.

As lowly writers, we only had contact with Dave Barry who was our boss and not with Wayne Newton, his boss.

We only saw Wayne for a few moments when he came on stage and Dave was finished.

We later learned that Dave would end his act the moment that Wayne had him signaled to hurry up and get off "his" stage.

And that was kind of how it went night after night.

No matter how good or interesting or fascinating the jokes were that we gave him, when Wayne decided he was ready to come out and take the stage, Dave Barry immediately had to wrap "it" up and get out of the way.

We enjoyed working from Dave's room. It was a pretty relaxed atmosphere where Dave sometimes would wait on us for a change.

Drinks and food were provided by the hotel, and we were treated like rock stars or at least Dave was. Whatever he wanted, he got and we sort of got his left-overs.

At this time, we did a lot of brain-storming. We would talk about what we had written earlier and what went over well and hopefully we could re-use some of the good stuff.

Then we would sit around with Dave and he would tell us his ideas and what area of life's comedy that he wanted us to explore.

He was always very encouraging even though he could be pretty rough on us at the same time.

He never let us forget that we were the hired help who were being paid to do a job, even though we were doing that job in Las Vegas.

Hopefully there would be something interesting in that? News that we could joke about.

Occasionally, there might be a scandal going on, and we would write about that.

Apparently, we were doing okay because we continued working.

After a few hours work in Dave's room, we were done for the day and then we would get to relax for a while and follow that up with a nice dinner in one of the main dining rooms.

After dinner, we would always head for the showroom.

I couldn't believe how many people were lined up for the evening shows. I knew it was Las Vegas, and that it was the show capital of the world, but I never realized how popular Wayne Newton was.

It was well over an hour before the doors would open up for the showroom and the seating, but the waiting line was sometimes all the way back through the entire casino. This guy was really popular.

My partner and I always got the best seats in the house.

We were in the closest row of seats to the stage where we listened carefully how Dave Barry would warm up the audience for Wayne Newton as he delivered our jokes.

We weren't there to necessarily enjoy the show as we were there to strictly observe what jokes of Dave's worked on the audience and what did not.

Our job was to calculate the reaction to the lines and fix up anything that didn't work for him.

Dave would stay on stage throwing out joke after joke until that little red light went off and then he would end his time with a few departing shots and walk off.

And so, on this eventful evening in our lives, my partner and I were sitting in the usual front row spot, making our notes and thinking up new and improved material for Dave's next stage appearance when Wayne made his usual smiling appearance with a fast-paced song or two.

At the end of the second song and while Wayne took a moment out to sip at a drink of water, we got up and excused ourselves from our seats and left through the kitchen doors by the side of the stage.

We didn't see Dave who sometimes waited for us so we continued walking through the kitchen and on into the casino floor.

We drifted over to watch the action at one of the crap tables as we waited for Dave to find us as he usually did.

A lot of time went by and Dave did not appear and we decided to try our hands at the crap table which, at that moment was having a hot run with lots of excitement being generated all around it.

Maybe an hour went by and my luck was still running really good, when suddenly everyone at the crap table stopped talking as they looked over our shoulders.

This part of the casino became the quietest spot anywhere as I looked around to see what everyone was looking at behind where we were standing against the crap table.

We turned around and noticed three huge security guards from the hotel standing there looking at my partner and myself.

Two of them had our luggage, and the third one came over and put his "paws" on my shoulder.

I told him who we were and he was not impressed. He then explained the reason for their appearance with our belongings.

"No one" he said "walks out on a Wayne Newton's performance. No one and you two broke the rule and walked out."

Apparently, Wayne Newton wanted to know who the two guys were who walked out in the middle of his show.

He was put off because these two guys had the best seats in the house and everyone in the room saw them get up and leave and that had never been done before.

As soon as he got off the stage, Wayne Newton did some detective work and finally approached Dave Barry.

So, when Dave told Wayne that we were his writers, Wayne's response was not anymore, they're not.

Not only were we done writing for Dave Barry, but we were banished from the hotel never to return.

At least, those were Wayne Newton's orders, and that was why there were three security guards and our luggage standing there next to us in the casino.

As we were being escorted from the Sands Hotel and Casino, I informed the guards that because of these actions on the part of Wayne Newton, that this hotel would come tumbling down and not survive without us in the town of Las Vegas.

And as time has shown, I was absolutely right.

The Sands Hotel and Casino stands no more. There's a new hotel where the Sands Hotel once stood, but I can't even tell which one it is.

They should have known better than to have us thrown out.

Action caused reaction. Wayne newton should have known better than to mess with me.

In the end, there was no winner. Nor was there really a loser.

The situation was just unfortunate and life went on for all of us.

20th CENTURY FOX STUDIOS AND THE HAPPY WANDERER

Frank Tarloff was my step-uncle.

He was one of the more respected writers of the sixties.

He had a group of friends that were responsible for such shows as *The Dick Van Dyke Show*, *The Andy Griffith Show*, and the *Danny Thomas Show*.

Unfortunately, he was one of the many "blacklisted" writers who couldn't use his own name to write material or in many instances, he just couldn't find work.

Fortunately for him, he had a lot of friends, so he always had the opportunity for work.

Whatever show he worked on, he just used a name other than his. He was very fortunate to have the connections that he had.

Frank also had an Academy Award for writing a Cary Grant comedy. *Father Goose* was his award-winning script.

This alone made sure that he always had a calling card whenever he talked to someone about writing their show. However, I only saw one problem with my step-uncle. He just was not a very nice guy to me.

He was rather curt and short tempered.

I never really knew if it was just me that he was nasty to, or if that was just the way he was. I'll never know.

When I was about fourteen or fifteen, I wrote a script and asked my uncle for his opinion.

At that time, he was working on a script for a movie that was being shot at 20th Century Fox Studios. It was called, *A Guide for the Married Man.*

I'm sure that he was under a lot of pressure because they were filming the movie while he was still writing it.

This wasn't the usual practice for a writer, but this movie was going to be as good as it could possibly be under these circumstances.

It had all the biggest comedians of the time and it had Gene Kelly as its director.

I sent Frank my script for a current television show, and he shot me off his criticism of my script almost immediately.

Frank sent me a very mean spirited reply to my script, and basically told me to find another profession.

Everything he stated was nasty. He didn't have one nice thing to say.

At least he could have said that my page count was nice, but that would have been too much to ask.

I was really hurt and disappointed at his words. He could have given me some helpful words, but he chose the latter.

It was at this time that I hit upon another idea.

If I could, I would use Uncle Frank for a lunch date at the studio.

He couldn't be nasty to me while we ate in the studio commissary. Too many of his friends and actors would be around.

He would have to introduce me to these people, and if I could, I would put them in my back pocket for a telephone call at a later date, or I might bump into them on the studio lot, and maybe I could possibly use them to help further my career.

At any rate, I would try and use my nasty uncle to help me in an unknowing way, because he certainly wouldn't do so if he knew what my plans were.

Finally, Uncle Frank Tarloff and I had a fixed lunch date. I arrived at the studio and went into the waiting area.

A security guard was in charge of letting people into the offices, and he was in charge of the buzzer which opened one of two doors.

The only other way into the studio grounds, was an open area where actors and studio personnel entered and exited.

Unfortunately, this area was heavily guarded and there was no way for me to sneak in.

Anyway, I waited for Uncle Frank to appear for over thirty minutes. I asked the guard to call his office once again, but he refused.

He had already called him twice and reminded me that Mr. Tarloff was aware that I was waiting for him.

"If I have to wait any longer," I told him, "We'll be having dinner and not lunch"; I said, but he was not amused by my attempt at humor.

He was used to people trying to sneak into the studio, and he's heard all sorts of excuses.

He had heard them all, and to him, I was just another star struck kid trying to see movie stars and the like.

Almost an hour went by when Frank finally appeared. The security guard hit the buzzer and I opened the door.

I felt like I had a pass into the Land of Oz.

I finally made it to the first step of my master plan.

Lunch with Uncle Frank was step number two.

That was when he said it. "I'm sorry I can't have lunch with you. I'm too busy in my office, but you can still have lunch."

"Just go to the commissary and get yourself something to eat. Their food isn't bad. Maybe we'll eat together another time, but probably not here. I'm too busy."

"Can we get together after lunch?" I asked.

"Sorry Ronnie. I'm too busy. You may have time to screw around, but I don't. I have a movie to work on. I can't waste any time on you, so after your lunch you should probably just leave."

These words crushed me. My whole plan was suddenly ruined.

If I couldn't have lunch with Uncle Frank and maybe meet some important people, what was I supposed to do?"

"Do you think it'll be all right if I walk around a little while and watch stuff being filmed outside?"

"Look Ronnie, here's the deal. I don't care what you do, but if anyone questions you, tell them that you snuck onto the lot."

"But, we were going to have lunch together. I'll just tell them that I came here to see you."

"No. Don't do that. I'm busy writing. Don't tell anyone you even know me."

"Just say what I told you. You got by security and you're lost. Ask for the way out."

"I have to go now.," and with that, my step-uncle walked away and left me standing in the hall of the administration building.

What a nasty man, I thought. Now what was I going to do?

I thought about leaving, but I remembered that I had a plastic pass which was pinned on my shirt pocket.

It meant that I could stay on the lot. I didn't know where it allowed me to wander, but I'll just grab something in the commissary and then walk around.

Maybe, I'll see a movie star or I'll meet someone who will put me into a movie. At any rate, today might be the most important day in my life.

On my way to the commissary, I came upon a sound stage that had a huge giant rocket in front of it.

I gathered up enough courage and opened the stage door. I was really afraid as I walked past a bunch of huge plants.

I thought that I would run into a studio guard who would throw me out, but that didn't happen.

As I became more at ease, I realized that this whole sound stage was full of giant plants. It was part of the *Planet of the Apes* movie. It was really cool.

I was alone in this huge building, and I could check out these plants which would look real on the silver screen, but in reality, were not real. I felt like a real tourist.

As I left the building, I ran into a security guard. He quickly looked at me.

"Is there something I can help you with?"

"Yes." I answered nervously. "Can you help direct me to the commissary?"

He was more than happy to, and he watched me as I followed his directions until I turned the corner. I kept walking until I turned another corner and I accidently found the commissary.

I decided to have something to eat and found a table for myself.

I couldn't believe how much everything cost, but I didn't care.

My table faced inward and I could see the entire room. I was sure that I would be able to spot anyone famous if they were in the building.

Then I saw him. It was a table for two with only one person eating by himself.

He was a famous guy all right. He was an Academy Award winner. He was my Uncle Frank. What an Asshole.

I knew that he didn't want to sit with me. But, maybe no one wanted to sit with him. That would be justice. Maybe a security guard will tell him to leave. Ha, ha!

Uncle Frank was unaware of my presence, and I didn't approach him.

I waited for him to leave before I left. I took a stroll between stages, and then I came upon a quiet street with a very famous car parked in front of an official building.

To my total delight, I was staring at the one and only, "Batmobile."

I looked around and around and saw no one as I got closer and closer to what would be the world's most famous car.

I got right up to the car and looked around again. Then I opened the door and got inside. As I closed the door, I heard a very annoyed voice.

"Hey. Get out of there."

I didn't know who yelled at me, but I got out of the car as fast as I could and closed the door. I hurriedly walked away.

"Keep walking," someone yelled as I left the area. I was happy that I wasn't being led away by a security guard.

I saw another stage door and the area didn't appear to be occupied.

I intended to enter when a red light suddenly started to flash above the door.

There was a sign next to it which stated that no one should enter while the red light was on. The light indicated that filming was taking place.

A security guard was headed my way and my heart started beating fast as he approached.

Then, the red light went off, and I entered the door and tried to blend in with a group of people who obviously worked on this show.

I starred at the door and didn't see it open so I felt quite safe.

Then, I looked around and realized that I was inside what appeared to be a submarine.

The people around me were busy doing their jobs, so no one paid attention to me.

Then a loud buzzer went off and someone yelled, "QUIET ON THE SET."

Then I saw some actors I recognized and realized that I was on the set of "*Voyage to the Bottom of the Sea.*"

I saw actors, Richard Basehart and David Hedison.

They were the stars of the show. My inclination was to ask for their autographs, but I wanted to blend into the workers instead of standing out as someone who should not be there, so I kept to myself and watched them film other scenes.

I became quite comfortable on the set and when they weren't filming, I walked around.

It was just like walking inside a real submarine. One corridor led to another corridor, and there were rooms or quarters off to the sides.

I followed one of the corridors, and it led me into the torpedo room which was really cool.

And right across from there was the control room, but I was looking at it from the opposite side of the thick glass.

It was filled with water which gave it a magnified look.

During the filming, they pumped a lot of air into the water

which filled the water with bubbles. It made the submarine appear as if it was going up or down. It was an early special effect.

After I saw everything that there was to see, I left the sound stage and wandered around until I happened onto the sound stage where they were filming Uncle Frank's movie.

I walked onto the set and saw the world-famous Gene Kelly.

Not only was he a famous actor, but he was the director on this movie.

I figured that this was the only place where I could use Uncle Frank's name to anyone questioning me.

But, no one did. I watched them film a couple of scenes and then I left.

It was a pretty full day, but I would come back another time and get there earlier so I could see more.

For some reason, I felt addicted to this place, and I couldn't get enough of it. There was so much to see and I couldn't wait to come back.

§

A few weeks later, I ditched school and showed up at the studio. Uncle Frank was surprised to hear that I was waiting to see him in the lobby. And after a long while, he came down.

We talked through the lobby door. He could see me through the glass.

"I don't have time to have lunch with you or give you a studio tour," he said.

"That's all right, Uncle Frank. If someone catches me on the lot, I'll just say that I snuck in. I promise I won't mention you."

And with those magic words, the buzzer went off, and I opened the door to my own private Disneyland. Uncle Frank turned and went back to his office.

I hurried down the stairs and onto the lot. I had told my friends in school, that I was at the studio, but no one believed me.

They told me that I was making up the whole thing. I knew that one day I'd have to prove to my friends that I really had a connection to the studio and that I could walk around as I pleased. At any rate, I had hoped that would be the case.

I'd do anything not to get caught and thrown out. That would mean that my friends were right and I just could not let that happen.

I knew my way to the set of "*Voyage to the Bottom of the Sea.*" I felt comfortable there.

Everyone was so friendly and I became friends with the script girl. It just so happened that she was the niece of Bud Abbott from Abbott and Costello, so we instantly had a connection which was my friend Bud who was her uncle.

We didn't talk much about Abbott and Costello because she was always busy and I respected that.

Besides, I didn't want to be a pest, especially to one of my first connections on the lot.

I tried to become friends with many of the actors on the show, but I was not sure if they knew that I really shouldn't be there or not. I don't think that they really cared one way or the other.

Then, I became brave enough to venture out into the sound stage next door.

There were no people on the premises so that made my venturing out that much more perfect.

When I got there it certainly looked very familiar to me.

I remembered that I had seen this stage used in one way or another on other shows such as, *Lost in Space*, *The Time Tunnel*, and *Voyage to the Bottom of the Sea* just to name a few.

I later learned that it was referred to as a tandem stage. In the sixties, a lot of shows shared this group of various second sets.

It was used quite a bit for Irwin Allen's other shows. It was a smart decision. A few changes here and there, and it became useful for other shows and movies.

§

Missing school was easy.

My parents were divorced and my mother worked full time, so there was really no one who kept track of me.

Believe it or not, several of the security guards at the studios became my dear friends. They would see me almost every day and they assumed that I belonged there.

I no longer needed my surly uncle to get through the security door. I simply walked right through the main entrance with the actors, extras, employees and the like.

The security guys always greeted me as I walked past their posts. I became a regular as I spent a lot of time wandering around the sets. I truly had my private Disneyland, didn't I?

On this particular day, early in my wandering time, I followed a kind of path that led to a small hill which housed three sound stages which were loosely connected to each other.

When I got to the first sound stage, I noticed that the main door was opened and I was stupefied at my find.

Inside this massive structure was the full-size spaceship for the television show, *Lost in Space*. This was the most expensive set for a television show. It cost $350,000 to build the entire ship with the second floor about thirty feet from the first floor. The rest of the set was devoted into making the rest of the area resemble another planet.. The ship also had a small space pod that was kind of a "Uber" for the ship. It carried a joke on the side. In easy to read numbers, it had the telephone number to 20th Century Fox - The very studio where the show was being filmed. And if that weren't enough, the "Lost in Space" Robot cost a small fortune as well.

No one was around, so naturally, I entered like I owned the lot.

I was spotted by a security guard, and my heart skipped a beat, but he remembered me from the entrance area, and he greeted me with a friendly smile, and a few kind words. He just continued on his rounds and I continued on mine.

I could not believe my good fortune. These people at the Studio had the laxest security I had ever seen, and I was eternally grateful. I had become the kid in the candy store.

But, I didn't want to press my luck too far, so I stayed out of view whenever possible and I didn't talk to many people.

If, on the rare occasion that I happened to see Uncle Frank in the distance, I made myself invisible and got out of sight.

I didn't know how he would react if he saw me on the lot, and I had no desire to find out.

§

Watching "Lost in Space" being filmed was the biggest treat of them all.

Up to that moment, I had only watched it on television, but now, everyone in the cast became very friendly with me.

Even Bob May, who was the man inside the "Robot" was my buddy.

The cast acted a little different around him because his face wasn't an on-camera actor.

Also, the producers wouldn't let Bob May's voice be the one heard on the show. Instead, famous announcer Dick Tufeld's voice was dubbed-in for the Robot's voice.

I can only remember one instance when Bob May's voice was used.

It happened when the Robot entered the scene with a guitar and he sang "Happy Birthday" to actress Angela Cartwright's character. Listening to Bob May sing reminded me why the producers of the show did not want his real voice to be heard.

The biggest break out star on the show turned out to be Billy Mumy. He played the part of young Will Robertson.

Billy and I were about the same age, and during the first year of the show, Billy attended Canfield Elementary School when he wasn't at the studio.

As a matter of fact, that's the very same Elementary School which I attended. Apparently, we both lived in or around the Pico area of Los Angeles. It was less than two miles from the studio.

Billy hung around with a different group of kids than I had.

These kids kissed his ass because he was a regular face on television.

He had not only acted on, *The Twilight Zone*, but he also had acted in several movies.

He was just a familiar face that everyone knew.

And now he was starring on a major television show.

When the program first started, the opening credits announced that Guy Williams, the star of *Zorro* was the main star, and the co-star was June Lockhart of *Lassie* fame.

Unfortunately for them, Dr. Smith, young Will, and the Robot, ended up becoming the most popular characters on the show.

Jonathan Harris who played the prissy villain, Dr. Smith, was always given a special announcement at the end of the show credits as being the "special guest star."

Well, that may have been the plan at the beginning of the show, but that didn't happen and the credits were never fixed.

The actors seemed to like one another just fine, but I'm sure there was some animosity between them.

On the set, it was easy to see that the main stars had become less of a force on the show and it wasn't their fault.

It was just how the show evolved. It was as if the show got turned around from where it had started.

And speaking of money, it became wide known that Groucho Marx made a fortune from the "Lost in Space" program as one of its initial investors.

Another interesting stroke of luck came my way. Comedian Red Skelton's brother was in charge of the Robot.

He knew that I liked it when Bob May would be taken out of the costume or put back inside the Robot.

One fateful day, he asked if I wanted to be placed into the Robot. WOW.

Naturally I jumped at the chance and in I went. I was instructed that I could not let anyone know that I was inside the Robot.

I was wheeled out onto the real set and they did one take as I remember. Why, I even smoked a cigarette while I was inside.

But, no one said a word, and I was nervous as all can be, while I was inside.

Then they shot the scene and I was taken into a far corner of the set and taken out of the Robot.

It was great. I then asked how much money I was going to get for doing this and I was told that the answer was nothing, since I could never tell anyone. Well, I thought that sucked but since I did not belong on the set, and I was invisible to one and all, I really had nothing to say and I let it all go away.

I later found out that Bob May who was supposed to be. inside the Robot, got paid for the scene.

When I told my friends that it really was me inside the Root for that scene, no-one believed me. I guess that was understandable.

One last observation on the *Lost in Space* set before I move on. In the corner of the set, all the guys would gather under one of the spot-lights and play a few hands of poker.

Whenever they did this Billy Mumy would come over with his guitar and climb up a small ladder and play some songs and sing.

Most of the card players would make faces at this but they did not say a word to him. You see, Billy was a star and they didn't want to jeopardize their jobs by complaining about something that Billy did.

And finally, here is my good-by to my fun studio days or as they say in the business—here is my final "Swan-Song" at the studio.

On the soundstage, next to the *Lost in Space* set, they were shooting a new series called *The Time Tunnel*.

It was a great time traveling series that starred teen heartthrob, James Darren.

Between filming, we used to sit around the set and talk.

One day he asked me what I wanted to do in life, and I replied that I wanted to be an actor to which he replied with a strong, "No! This is not a good idea."

Forget acting he told me. "If you want to get in front of the camera, you need to become a writer. Then you can write yourself a part and keep it going until you become a star."

Then he flung a "Time Tunnel" script on my lap.

"Here," he said. Start by writing one of these shows and then go from there.

James Darren's words made a lot of sense and so I started to write. I gave up on acting and settled for a typewriter.

For my first script, I picked *The Time Tunnel*, of course. But no matter how good it might have been, it didn't matter.

The show only lasted one season and I went back to school.

But before that happened, I had to contend with my disbelieving schoolmates who thought my stories about the studio were all made up.

My friends just didn't believe the stories I told them about going to the studios so I decided to take my best friend with me on one of my adventures.

His name was Mark and before Gary Marshal came up with the character Fonzie for his *Happy Days* television program, I had my own Fonzie.

My Fonzie/Mark wore blue jeans, a white t-shirt and had a pack of cigarettes under his sleeve. He was the perfect role model for the Fonz.

Within a few days, I took Mark to the outside set where they were filming the pilot for the show *Nanny and the Professor*.

On that particular day, I was wearing a suit and tie because I had some ideas that I was going to give to one of my new contacts at the studio.

We were hanging around the *Nanny and the Professor* set so that I could show Mark how it was done when the director who obviously did not know our faces, came over and asked me if I was working on this set.

Of course, I said yes and since I was wearing a suit and tie, he placed me in the background with some other properly dressed guys.

Then he walked over to Mark who looked just the opposite of everyone else who was there and questioned him.

Well, Mark was never a good liar, and before long both Mark and I were escorted by security off the lot, and told never to come back again and that was my final time of crashing into the studio.

Down the road and into the future, of which I had no way of knowing at that time, I would be welcomed through the front door and have a place of my own in this very special world of make believe.

GOOD TIMES
ANOTHER NORMAN LEAR SHOW

In the 1970's we had the very good fortune of having several ground breaking television shows.

All in the family," was the story of a bigot, Archie Bunker, living in queens with his submissive wife and their daughter who married the very opposite of her father.

You might call the son-in-law a "card carrying hippie."

This show became such a hit that it spawned several more shows.

The first spin-off was *The Jefferson's*.

The Jefferson's was a show about the Bunker's black neighbors.

These neighbors made frequent appearances on *All in the Family*, as did Archie Bunker's cousin, his female counterpart "Maude."

Both shows, *The Jefferson's* and *Maude* went on and into their own shows.

The final spin-off was with Ester Rolle, who played Maude's maid. Its title was *Good Times*," but its title didn't exactly fit the show.

It was the story of a poor family living in the tenements of Chicago and who were about as poor as dirt.

The daughter was a very outgoing and bright girl.

The older of two boys was a comical idiot who always looked on the bright side of the worst of times.

But he did have a catch-phrase, when he said the word, "Dyno-mite!"

Whenever he said it, the audience always applauded and there was a beat of silence.

He was allowed to say it only twice an episode.

Just like Fonzie on *Happy Days*, he was allowed to say "Ayyyy." But also, only twice an episode.

The youngest *Good Times* son, Michael, was a bright kid and student who always tried to help the family.

But it was the father who was the head of the family. That is when his wife let him.

But he did have the loudest voice, and he truly was the king of his castle.

I came on the show about the. 4th season.

I was delighted that I was going to write on a show that featured John Amos.

However, as it turned out, John Amos had left the show to co-star in a mini-series called, *Roots*.

On our *Good Times* show we had to write John Amos out of the show, and so in the opening episode we had John's character killed off in Alaska.

The offices for *Good Times* were being remodeled. Our studio was across the street from Channel 5 on Sunset Blvd.

It had many stages where many shows were filmed using studio audiences.

They even filmed some game shows there. The reason I bring up the location of the studio, is because it's not there anymore.

For some reason, the property was sold, and now a high school sports area stands in its place. You can't miss it.

Anyway, while our offices were being redone, I had to go back and forth between the studio and home where I did most of the work on the script.

In the beginning, I went in to see the producers with my partner. We had several ideas for the episodes which were all shot down, except for one that they liked.

Everyone in the room helped us mold that idea into a workable show, and we went home to put the pieces together from our notes.

Funny thing though, since we had no regular offices, the studio rented a room across the street at the Dunes Motel.

Now, this motel was not a regular Hollywood Motel with· your everyday tourists.

No... no... no... It was a motel of prostitution.

We would walk upstairs to the offices of *Good Times*, and on either side of us were rooms where people were coming and going by the hour.

It was a little hard (excuse the pun) to get our work done when we knew that any minute the police might show up and raid us.

We had a pretty good reason for being there so that we could write our show and all that, but I worried that we could be found guilty by our just being there.

On the way up to the offices, I was often accosted by a dealer who offered me cocaine or a hooker to spend time with.

Most of the rooms at the motel were rented out by the hour.

These guys never did figure it out that we were using a room as a production office.

We really didn't have much time for such nonsense.

A lot of unwanted customers, the girls or their handlers, would often walk into our production office because the door was always open. I guess it looked like another place for them to do their business.

After a few weeks of putting up with all of this, my partner and I decided to get to work at home.

Needless to say, that Hollywood Motel was quite a strange place to put a bunch of Hollywood big shot writers trying to put on a weekly show.

I don't remember us getting much of anything done while we were there.

Fortunately, the show came out great thanks to my partner and me.

We received a lot of compliments on the episode but unfortunately, after that one show, my partner and I split up our partnership and we went our separate ways.

It was sad because Bruce and I had been friends since High School and we had many great years together.

Looking back, I wish that we had stayed together, but that's show-biz.

And speaking of show-biz, one day, we heard that Orson Wells, that great actor, was coming to the studio.

Everyone was excited, and we all wanted to meet him. Luckily, I caught a glimpse of him going into Norman Lear's office. I was surprised at how big a man he was, but I was glad that I got to see him.

ALL IN THE FAMILY

All in the Family was the biggest show of its day.

There was always standing room only whenever the shows were being taped. The production area was always packed with the public who could never get enough of our show.

One of the nicest people I had ever met in Hollywood was Carol O'Connor.

He liked to talk to me when they weren't taping.

He had a lot of ideas about future shows, and he liked to try out his ideas on me.

He was a very likeable man, and I always got along with him as I did with the rest of the cast.

However, Rob Reiner was a different sort.

He just seemed aloof. He had his own set of friends and sometimes they came by and sometimes they didn't.

I knew Rob since we were kids. We used to go to a hot-dog joint called Flooky's.

It had batting cages and we'd all take turns on one of the fast pitch batting cages. As I remember it, he always hogged the cage and that always pissed me off.

Anyway, back to *All in the Family*.

Things were going swimmingly and the shows were being taped on a steady basis.

After the taping everyone would retire to their dressing rooms to receive guests.

I used to walk down the hallway to see which Hollywood stars had showed up to visit. It was interesting to see which dressing room the visiting stars would pop into and out of.

The first door on the left was always filled with a lot of great food and drinks.

Then down the hallway I would walk with a drink in my hand watching everything that was going on.

Everyone's room was crowded and people were standing in the hallway waiting for their turn to get into the dressing rooms.

Every room that is, but Rob Reiner's.

I remember him standing in his doorway waiting for someone to visit him. But I guess his friends weren't there or maybe he just wasn't that friendly to everyone.

However, all in all, it was a wonderful experience on the set and afterwards, and I always had a blast.

I later wrote an episode for the show which got me a job on an ABC special.

I had a six-month contract and boy was that an experience.

ABC STUDIOS IN HOLLYWOOD

My agent finally came through and got me a job on an ABC special.

My contract was for six months and I couldn't have been happier.

The man in charge was Danny Simon. He was the brother of the great Neil Simon.

When I met Danny, he told me that he hired me on the strength of my *All in The Family* script which one of his readers had passed on to him.

Everything seemed great until Danny told me that I had a writing partner.

I reminded him that I always worked alone and he agreed to that.

I would write almost all of the material by myself, but on the papers with the studio, I had a partner.

This allowed him to hire two writers for the price of one. I would have to split my salary with a complete stranger.

He also told me that there were four other writers on the show, and they had to split their salaries also.

I did most of my work for ABC at home. If I was at the studio, I knew that my old habit of just wandering around would get me, so I tried not to go there.

ABC was not a huge movie studio as some of the other locals were. It was more of a small studio surrounded by a local housing development.

I could more accurately describe it as a television studio and not a movie studio. The size is what differed one from the other.

Whenever I was at ABC, I used to enjoy wandering on stage, and watch from the side of the stage where they would tape the local news broadcasts.

There was one special person at the ABC studio that I loved to watch.

He was the stations weather man who happened to have been an experienced meteorologist and not just an announcer with a pretty face.

He seemed to love his work and he was absolutely passionate about it. He explained everything that was going to happen in great detail and he was easy to understand.

He had great ratings for his program as the people of Los Angeles and I loved to watch and listen to him.

He was great fun to watch.

Since I took meteorology in college, Dr. George and I had a lot to talk about.

He was truly a terrific man who loved what he did. We don't have that today and it is too bad.

Instead, we have a lot of good-looking women who stand in front of the facts and figures.

The best that we can do is pretty much guess what the weather will be.

I don't mind looking at these babes, but I do miss my friend Dr. George.

The ABC slogan at that time was "Still the One." This was the same title as the song that was out there by the singing group called "Orleans."

Every network station had its own slogan and this interesting one was theirs.

I continued to take my daily walks around the studio at my lunch times. One time I stumbled onto a kind of party set up.

All the tables were decked out as if there was going to be a large party. It was obvious that they were getting ready to start filming shortly.

What I found to be most interesting was the sign hanging from the ceiling.

It said, "Dick Clark's Rockin' New Year's Eve."

It was pretty interesting except that New Year's Eve was still six months away and this entire set seemed very familiar to me. I knew that I had seen something like it during my early wandering days at another location.

I hung around on the stage area until I saw some of the crew filtering in.

It was explained to me that they were going to film the party now and play it back on New Year's Eve.

This all sounded familiar to me as they went from present time to future time and no one would be able to tell that they were shot on different days.

I wasn't happy about finding out all this detailed information because I had been watching Dick Clark's show for years and years.

I wasn't happy finding out that I had been tricked as a viewer all this time.

However, now that I was an insider and knew how all these things really worked, I sort of thought that it made some sort of sense.

I guess that makes me a hypocrite, but, that was okay, because, after all, that was Hollywood.

WRITING CARTOONS

I went to the Los Angeles Writer's Guild West office for a trial.
In television, there are a lot of people who take your ideas and stories and use them as their own.

That's one way they get rich and it is not uncommon.

It is always the writer that gets ripped off.

He does not get the glory, the credit or the fame from his work.

And above all, he may never make it in his chosen profession if this keeps happening to him.

Anyway, while I was in the waiting room at the Guild, I met a very nice gentleman.

He was a writer too. As it turned out, he was there for the same reason that I was there.

His material and hard work had been ripped off by the same guy.

We became fast friends. We had a lot in common.

While I had been working in television, he worked in animation where he would write cartoons.

My new friend Buzz, had been ripped off by the very same guy who stole my ideas.

This guy would have gotten away with stealing from Buzz, but this culprit, who we shall call Sammy Glick, violated several Writer's Guild Rules and whenever this happens, the Writer's Guild always steps in with free attorney services for guys like us as they take on the cases.

I wish to take a moment to explain why I decided to call the bad guy in this situation "A Sammy Glick."

This name comes from the antagonist of Budd Schulberg's novel, *What Makes Sammy Run.*

In the novel, Sammy Glick is a heartless go-getter who will stop at nothing to pursue his personal ambitions, regardless of the consequences to others.

Thus, "A Sammy Glick" is a person who exemplifies these same personality traits.

TO CONTINUE: If there is one thing a Writer's Guild Member better not do, is to violate the rules of the Guild.

And that's exactly what Sammy Glick had done.

Oddly enough, that is what happened both to Buzz and to me.

Sammy Glick had multiple meeting with me and picked my brain and stole several ideas from me.

He would call me back time and time again. I thought I was, going to get hired onto his show, but that was never the case.

So, when I informed the guild what had transpired, they informed me that I had a case against Mr. Glick.

So, here I was with Buzz. Fortunately, Buzz came out and told me that he had just won his case against Sammy, and now it was my turn.

I walked into a room full of attorneys and told my story.

My Guild attorney had a few words to say and then the attorney for Universal stood up and called Sammy Glick a thief for stealing my ideas and using them. I was delighted.

Not only did I win my case, but I found a new writing partner with Buzz.

Buzz brought me along to Hanna Barbara Studios. They were the biggest animation house in the country.

Buzz immediately found me work there and I found myself with a job.

I worked on *Scooby Doo*, *Mork and Mindy*, and *The Smurfs*, along with many more.

My last assignment was at Marvel Productions where they did such things as *The Incredible Hulk*, among others.

I remember when Buzz and I had been working on a *Mork and Mindy* script.

We were half way done with it when the telephone rang. It was the studio.

They wanted the two of us to come right down to the studio to talk about *Mork and Mindy*. We were nervous as hell but we tried not to let it show.

We arrived at the studio ready to defend our positions on our work but we weren't sure what this was all about.

Buzz and I walked into a conference room full of seated people. The heads of the *Mork and Mindy* show were all there watching us as we took our seats.

We felt all the eyes upon us as Buzz and I whispered back and forth. We decided to have a united front and stand behind whatever we had written for them already.

"So, what do you have ready for us?" the producer asked with a broad smile on his face.

"What do you mean?" Buzz queried.

We need another show from you guys, and we need it almost immediately." He replied.

The other people in the room chimed in.

It seemed that we were being asked there today, for us to tell them about our next episode for the show.

I guess we were the only ones who knew there was no other episode being worked on. We were just finishing up the one that we had already given them.

"So, what's the next show going to be about?" the same spokesman asked.

All that Buzz and I could do was to talk in circles. Then out of plain nervousness, we made up a running story and everyone in the room helped us turn it into a real episode.

They gave us a bit of an idea and we jumped on it and they listened and added their input and things began going along very nicely.

We were just so relieved that we weren't getting fired and we actually enjoyed that meeting.

We finally left the room with another assignment under our belts and we laughed with each other all the way home.

When Buzz and I got back to our current script, I had an idea for Mork. It was a joke that to me just seemed perfect for this episode.

Buzz, however, didn't think it was funny and he didn't want to use it in this episode of the show.

However, we finally compromised.

Buzz agreed to use my joke if I would let one of his off-color jokes stay in.

So, that was what we did and when I saw my joke on television, I realized that Buzz was right. My joke was not that funny.

Scooby Doo was my most important piece of animation.

You see, Scooby had been around for years and I knew that it would always be on television.

So, I had to do the best job that I had ever done. It didn't matter that it was only a cartoon. It just had to be my best work ever.

This show probably would be on the air for generations and generations to come, and I wanted it to be just right.

So, I took my time on this project and I did get it right. The only problem that I encountered with it was when the studio told me that a shrinking ray that I used in the episode, couldn't look like a gun. (It was a very strange time in our business).

Children's programming was under strict control at that time.

A panel of educators at UCLA had to approve all ideas that involved children in case there was violence involved.

I now laugh when I think about today's ever-present violence on television and on video games.

HOLLYWOOD AGENTS

On every Hollywood agent's business card, it should real, "I was just going to call you."

That is their mantra or standard text line.

You could have an agent for weeks, months or years and the second you call them, you hear the familiar, "I was just thinking of you and I was getting ready to call you."

Their bull-shit never stops once it begins.

You can only get an agent if someone recommends one to you.

Calling an agent you heard about and telling them that you wrote the next best seller or you've appeared on Broadway won't do it. You'll get hung up on right after you announce why you're calling.

If you find someone who's just starting out, you don't have a chance?

If you don't know anyone and they don't know anyone either, you're on equal footing.

Polly was my first agent. She had great things planned for me. But it was a no-go.

I never heard from her unless I called her. "I was just thinking of you, for the 'blah - blah' show. But when I got a job, she was right there for her ten percent cut from off the top.

You see, a lot of agents sign a lot of people and hope that they'll get work on their own, and then the agent will get their percentage.

But, that's not always true.

Some agents do work really hard. At least that's what I always hear about them. I still have not seen it.

My partner Buzz had a different agent than me. It was one of the biggest companies, CAA or Creative Artists Agency.

I told Buzz about an idea I had for a movie. And to my surprise, Buzz got real excited and encouraged me to write it.

However, it was just an idea and' I really didn't want to do it until Buzz convinced me. So, we wrote it together.

"*Terror in Paradise*" was the title and that says it all. To this day, I believe that the title is responsible for selling the movie.

"*Terror in Paradise*" wasn't a typical movie.

We tried to make it a good, action movie. Sure, we had a girl running around topless, but she was supposed to have big breasts. In the movie, she was as small as she could be.

Before the movie got made, I had shown it to a few people.

Everyone was impressed with the structure and especially the ending.

The actor, "Chuck Connors" of the "Rifleman Television Show" and lately of many commercials, gave me a letter that stated that if the movie got made, he wanted to be in it as the bad guy.

I also got letters of intent from different actors, but that didn't matter.

The producers did their own thing and filmed the movie without any input from Buzz or myself. We were deeply disappointed.

To get our script made, Buzz and I gave copies of the script to our agents.

My agent told me the usual and that was that she found it interesting.

Buzz, however had an agent who actually came through.

She got an option on our script and they ended up making our movie. It took only a few weeks to get actors to sign up for parts and they went forward.

Naturally, my agent Polly who did nothing for me. or the movie, had gotten ten percent.

She got her ten percent and when I asked her why, she told me the truth. It was because she was thinking about me.

A few years later, I had written another script. As always, I didn't have an agent but I remembered Buzz and his agent CAA.

I telephoned them, but could not get past the girl on the switchboard.

It didn't matter that they had sold my first movie.

They hung up on me as fast as they could. You get treated better when you call a wrong number.

WRITING FOR TELEVISION

THIS IS A SHORT CHAPTER AND WE ARE WRITING IT IN ALL CAPITAL LETTERS.

WHY?

POSSIBLY IT IS BECAUSE WE DO NOT WANT YOU THE READER TO THINK THAT BEING A WRITER IS EASY.

OF COURSE, SITTING AT HOME AND WRITING A SCRIPT FOR A TELEVISION SHOW AND THEN SENDING IT IN SEEMS TO BE A PIECE OF CAKE DOESN'T IT.

UNFORTUNATELY, TELEVISION SHOWS HAVE RULES THAT HAVE TO BE FOLLOWED BECAUSE THEY JUST WILL NOT OPEN UP UNSOLICITED MANUSCRIPTS FROM JUST ANYONE.

IF YOU GIVE THEM A FRIENDLY FOLLOW UP CALL, YOU'LL END UP ONCE AGAIN TALKING TO YOURSELF BECAUSE THEY'VE PROBABLY ALREADY HUNG UP ON YOU.

THEY DO THESE THINGS TO PROTECT THEMSELVES. SUPPOSE YOU SEND IN SOMETHING AND SOMEHOW OR OTHER IT DOES END UP ON TELEVISION OR SOME OTHER WORTHWHILE VENUE, THEY'LL NEVER ADMIT THAT YOU WERE THE ONE WHO WROTE IT.

YOUR SIMILAR IDEAS WERE JUST A MERE COINCIDENCE.

THEY WILL TELL YOU OVER AND OVER THAT THEY NEVER OPENED UP YOUR MAIL, AND NO MATTER WHAT IT WAS THAT YOU WROTE, IT WAS ONE OF THEIR STAFF WRITERS WHO THOUGHT OF THE IDEA FIRST.

IF THEY STAY ON THE TELEPHONE LONG ENOUGH WITH YOU, THEY'LL TELL YOU THAT YOU NEED TO GET YOURSELF AN AGENT AND THAT SOUNDS EASY ENOUGH SO YOU GET A LIST OF AGENTS AND BEGIN DIALING.

AND WITH NO CREDITS AND NO NAMES TO DROP, YOU GET NOWHERE.

PACK UP YOUR THINGS AND HEAD EAST. GET THE HELL "OUT OF DODGE."

OR … YOU COULD BE SMART AND PLAY THE GAME "THEIR WAY."

START JOINING WRITING GROUPS.

MAKE FRIENDS AND BULL-SHIT YOUR WAY AROUND TOWN.

BY TOWN, WE MEAN HOLLYWOOD AND SUNSET BLVD.

LIE YOUR ASS OFF ABOUT WHO YOU ARE, AND WHAT YOU'VE DONE.

HOLLYWOOD PEOPLE RESPECT THAT.

WHY, HALF THE PEOPLE IN WEST LOS ANGELES ARE IN SHOW BUSINESS, OR IT LEAST THEY CLAIM TO BE.

AND HOPEFULLY, IF YOU PLAY THE GAME LONG ENOUGH, SOMEONE WILL TELL YOU THAT THEY HAVE AN AGENT WHO YOU CAN CALL TO SEE IF THEY WILL REPRESENT YOU, OR AT LEAST THEY HAVE SOMEONE WHO WILL LOOK AT SOMETHING YOU HAVE WRITTEN.

THAT, MY FRIEND IS A BEGINNING AND A POSSIBLE STARTING POINT.

AND AS MUCH AS YOU HATE PLAYING THAT GAME, IT IS THE ONLY ONE IN TOWN.

MAKE FRIENDS … EVEN PHONY ONES. YOU NEVER

KNOW WHEN THEY CAN GET YOUR CAREER GOING.

WHEN YOU FINALLY MEET IMPORTANT PEOPLE, THEY'LL WANT TO SEE YOUR RESUME SO START LYING.

THESE PEOPLE WILL LIE BACK TO YOU AND YOU WILL BE ON EVEN FOOTING.

AND WHEN YOU TELL THEM ABOUT WHAT YOU'VE DONE YOU'D BETTER HAVE A LOT OF CHOICES AND EVEN SOME SORT OF MOVIE CREDIT.

YOU NEVER KNOW WHAT WILL CLICK AND WHAT WON'T. IF IT DOESN'T WORK OUT RIGHT AWAY, THAT PERSON MIGHT REMEMBER YOU OR YOUR NAME AND SOMETIME IN THE FUTURE, YOU JUST MIGHT GET A JOB. AND THEN IT ALL BECOMES WORTH IT. BELIEVE ME.

IF YOU ARE REALLY LUCKY, YOU MIGHT RUN INTO SOMEONE WHO CAN HELP YOU.

MAYBE YOU'VE SEEN THEM ON TELEVISION OR IN THE MOVIES AND THEY'RE A GREAT PERSON READY TO GIVE SOMETHING BACK.

IT DOES HAPPEN. I'VE SEEN A LOT OF GREAT PEOPLE FOR A FEW MOMENTS.

I REMEMBER I WAS STANDING OUTSIDE AN ELEVATOR WAITING FOR IT TO OPEN AND THEN CAROL BURNETT WALK.ED OUT.

I SAID "HELLO" AND SHE SAID IT BACK TO ME. THAT MIGHT HAVE BEEN MY BIG CHANCE, BUT IT CAME AND WENT.

ANOTHER TIME AT 20TH CENTURY FOX, I RAN INTO SHIRLEY MCCLAIN. I TOLD HER WHAT A BIG FAN I WAS OF HERS AND SHE BLEW ME OFF.

SHE MUST HAVE HAD A BAD DAY OR SOMETHING. THAT DIDN'T EXACTLY HELP MY DAY EITHER.

SANDY KOUFAX

&

PETE ROSE

Sandy Koufax never intended on becoming a baseball player.

Basketball was his game.

He played for the University of Cincinnati.

Then one fateful day, he found out that the college baseball team was traveling to Florida for several games, and Sandy who didn't want to pass up a free trip to Florida, joined the baseball team.

At this point, I refuse to say anything silly like, "And the rest is history."

I know and have met Sandy Koufax on a personal basis many times, and I have never run into anyone who had an unkind word concerning him.

Even in today's world, people attending Dodger Stadium baseball games, still wear Koufax jerseys to honor him.

Sandy is considered to be possibly the greatest pitcher of all time.

While playing with the Dodgers, Koufax received respect from almost all the fans in the various ball parks, no matter what city he was in.

If the Dodgers were on a road trip, Sandy would come out to begin his warm-ups.

Then, something odd would occur.

The fans from the opposing team would give Sandy a standing ovation.

This was always embarrassing for Sandy, but he had to get used to it.

Even today, he doesn't like talking about it, because it's embarrassing, and he's not that type of guy.

I'm happy to say that Sandy Koufax is a friend of my family's. My Uncle used to call him in the morning and refer to him as "SAN-DA-LA."

I always thought that was pretty cool that he knew him that well that he had a nick name for him.

Sandy was a very giving man.

I remember when I wanted my 12-year-old son to learn how to throw the curve ball. And who better to learn it from than the master himself.

So, after several minutes of pleading, Sandy agreed to show him the proper way to hold the ball and throw it so that it would curve.

This advice came with my promise that he would not be allowed to use it during a game while he was so young.

Sandy knew that someone that young could only cause damage to their arm unless the curve ball was thrown one hundred percent correctly and that was almost impossible.

As a proud father, I was delighted that Sandy had instructed Scotty in the art of throwing the curve ball.

We all agreed that when Scotty entered the latter years of High School, he could use the "Koufax Curve."

We all realized that this kind of knowledge would have to be used by Scotty when he was old enough and trained enough so as to throw it properly and not hurt himself.

During one High School game, with two strikes on the batter, Scotty threw a beautiful curve ball.

The batter swung his bat and the curve did its thing. The batter glared at my son as he could not believe what the pitcher had been able to do with that last pitch.

The batter just dropped the bat on home plate and continued to stare at Scotty until the umpire made him pick up his bat and head into the dugout.

As a father, that was one of my proudest moments.

§

Whenever Scotty pitched and his team won the game, the newspaper announced that "such and such" team lost to the "Koufax Curve."

You see, the reporter for the paper was a huge Koufax fan and he had looked for any reason to use Sandy Koufax's name in his article.

It appeared that my son Scott, had learned from the ultimate teacher, and he really did know how to throw a Sandy Koufax pitch correctly.

Unfortunately, Sandy Koufax himself had to pay a price whenever he would continue to throw that pitch.

After each ball game that he pitched, he would have to soak his elbow in a bucket of ice for forty-five minutes.

Ultimately, all the pain that he had to endure in that elbow shortened Sandy's career as a big-league pitcher.

As great a pitcher as Sandy was, the same can't be said about his trips to the plate as a batter.

Sandy Koufax was an awful batter.

If he hit a foul ball, the crowd would roar as if he got a hit.

They were just grateful that he was able to hit the ball anywhere.

And when Sandy would get a hit, it was as if he had hit a grand slam.

Sandy had no trouble laughing at himself. He knew he wasn't a good batter.

He usually expected to strike out, and if he did, he'd walk slowly back to the dugout, and he would be smiling all the way.

No one ever rushed him as he retreated back to the bench.

And, if he made the third out of the inning, no one rushed him as he slowly made his way back to the pitcher's mound.

Koufax was given more time than anyone else to get back to the mound and get ready to pitch another inning.

Everyone who had a love for the game of baseball also had a strange affinity for the Dodger who wore number 32.

PETE ROSE

He went by many names.

He was known as Charlie Hustle or just The Hit King. And those were the nice names.

The Good Names.

Pete has been trying to get his good name restored by the baseball commissioner every year, but up to this moment this has not happened.

The case of Pete Rose remains an enduring scandal 26 years after the Cincinnati Reds player and manager agreed to a lifetime ban from Major League Baseball on August 23, 1989.

Pete feels to this day that he should be given a chance to become a Hall of Fame player.

Surely, he made a mistake by betting against his own team to win baseball games.

But, it wasn't just as simple as that.

As the manager of the Cincinnati Reds, he could control the outcome of the team games more than any one person.

His gambling was just out of control and he could not help himself, or so he said.

I met Pete Rose in 1999.

He was hiring himself out as an entertainment figure for one day contracts whenever he could get hired.

When I spent time with Pete, he was hired for the day at the Colorado Auto Auction in Denver, Colorado.

He would spend the day around hundreds of car dealers, and give them the opportunity to purchase a baseball signed by him for eight dollars.

Pete seemed to have a good time.

He was treated like a Rock Star.

Anyone could spend a few private minutes in the auction manager's office with Pete if they wanted.

However, on this day, I had one of my young sons with me, and we were allowed to lock the door to the office and spend almost an entire hour just talking with the great Pete Rose.

Once we told Pete that we were almost family with Sandy Koufax, we had Pete's undivided attention.

A lot of people wanted to come into that office on that day, but Pete told them they'd have to wait.

You see, Pete Rose was one of the people who had the experience of hitting against Sandy Koufax.

Pete immediately started off our conversation by talking about himself.

He said he was one of the greatest hitters in the history of the game.

He knew that he had made mistakes and he was now paying for them.

He did feel that he would one day get into the Baseball Hall of Fame but he thought that it would have to wait until he had passed away.

But, he said that he still was trying to move things forward but that it was a tough road.

I could tell that here was a man who truly felt remorseful about the major mistakes he had made.

Pete shifted gears and began talking about Sandy Koufax.

He made it a point to let us know that at the time he was playing the game, there was no pitcher that he could not get a hit off of.

However, when it came to Sandy Koufax, that was a completely different story.

Pete seemed to enjoy talking about Sandy's curve ball.

He explained that getting a hit off of a Koufax curve did not make you a great hitter. It just meant that you got "lucky."

That's how Pete felt. He had great respect for Koufax and nothing could ever change that.

He felt honored to have played during the Koufax era.

And regardless what happens with his own personal life, he'll always be one of the lucky ones who played against Sandy Koufax and the Los Angeles Dodgers.

Pete then gave us a most interesting demonstration of trying to hit a Koufax curve ball.

Pete took an ash tray on the desk and slowly pushed it off the edge.

Of course, the ash tray simply dropped straight down to the carpet.

"See," Pete said. "even if you knew it was coming, you couldn't hit the ball that was falling straight down."

"There I was, possibly with one of the best hitters in the game, and all I could do was watch that dammed ball drop like a dead weight right over the home plate."

"The Man had the greatest curve ball in the history of the game, and I should know because I was possibly the greatest hitter of all time. And yet, I couldn't touch a Sandy Koufax thrown curve ball."

COMBAT

In the 1960's, there was a television show, *Combat.*

It concerned the exploits of a squad of soldiers in France during World War II.

The Sergeant was the star of the show and everything he did affected everyone else. They all depended on him.

Over the several seasons that the show was on, they had plenty of guest stars.

Until one season, they had a special star.

It was Lee Marvin.

Mr. Marvin had done a lot of movies, but one thing that no one else on the show could claim was that they were wounded at Guadalcanal as he was. Guadalcanal was one of the biggest battles of the Second World War.

This went ahead and made Lee Marvin so very special on a show about soldiers. It was his badge of honor for the cast.

Everyone was just intimidated by who he was. It was nothing personal that he did, but he was Lee Marvin, after all.

He was a great guy and was very relaxed on the set, but yet he seemed to be bigger than life to everyone around him.

No one on the set could act just right.

The actors weren't themselves. Even the co-stars had a difficult time with Lee.

He was more than just a Hollywood Movie Star. He was someone who was actually in the real war, and it made everyone around him feel phony as they acted out the scenes and pretended that they were in World War II.

It was a hard episode to shoot. The scenes took longer and everyone watched Lee, so that they could do things just like he did. They wanted to look authentic.

Finally, the episode had been shot, and Lee Marvin moved on to other things.

However, he did have a lingering effect. A lot of the actors started holding their weapons like Lee and tried to even walk like him.

They all wanted to look like the real deal.

The reason I bring this up so many years later, is to remind you that not everyone can be a big-time Hollywood star and no one can be someone else.

I have been fortunate to have met a lot of interesting people at their very best and at their very worst.

And looking back, I realize that I have loved them all.

Well, maybe not all, but close.

I've seen what fame does and what regret can do. They are two vastly different animals.

As you read this, my adventures through my life will continue, and as my long time and very dear friend Bud Abbott used to say to me:

"Ron, may you live as long as you want, and never want as long as you live."

What a great saying that is, and I want to close my personal adventures here, with one final short story about a place, in southern California called the "Iverson Ranch."

THE IVERSON RANCH

The Iverson Ranch is located in the far west corner of the San Fernando Valley, which is a suburb of Los Angeles.

It is about thirty miles North from Hollywood itself, but this dusty patch of land with its sandstone rock formations, is the place where dreams were created and the make-believe was launched.

All the major film studios in recent times, and often in their far past, have settled down on the dusty trails of this area and made some of the most famous movies of all time.

If you would spend a night camping out in the area, you could probably easily imagine hearing six-shooters going off from the old days of stage coach robbers and actual gun fights that happened in the streets all around the area.

You can hear Chuck Connors, *The Rifleman* plying his trade and you can hear Hoss and Little Joe Cartwright defending some poor family that the bad guys are trying to run out of "their" town.

But, if you are really good, and really lucky, you can imagine seeing John Wayne stopping a stagecoach just to get a ride. (but we shall talk about this great scene that was really recorded here, a little later in this chapter).

As we all should know, the Iverson Family moved from the East Coast and established themselves as potato farmers on forty acres of land in 1908.

Driving North up Topanga Canyon Blvd. or Highway 27 as it is also named by the California Transit Authority, someone should point out to you a huge vacant lot that can be seen from the freeway.

This was the actual location of a great War Movie called the "*Green Berets.*"

If you look a little farther out, and from left to right, you can picture the masked man and his trusty Indian companion as the Lone Ranger would ride Silver as they went around the bend looking to find the bad guys.

Or maybe you can even remember the spot-location where you saw the first-ever-filmed Superman, staring George Reeves, as the Man of Steel, doing a quick-change and coming back as the greatest hero with a letter on his chest.

I love the Superman episode where Lois and Jimmy were stuck in an old western town run by a gun toting bad-guy.

Lois called Clark Kent for help and Clark just laughed it off until Lois said that the bully was making advances upon her.

Hearing this, Clark Kent ran down the hall at the Daily Planet where he worked as a mild-mannered reporter, and then flew out to rescue Lois and Jimmy from this gunslinger.

As Lois and Jimmy talked to Superman on the street of the Western town, I could not but help noticing that the background were the hills of Chatsworth, California. This is a place familiar to me because I call the greater area around it "home."

Yes, this and much more was all part of the Iverson history.

. As a matter of fact, the Iverson Ranch is the most widely filmed outdoor location in the entire world.

As I said, it is located in a remote comer of the San Fernando Valley on the outskirts of Los Angeles.

It was the central hub of the outdoor movie business from the 1930's to the 1950's.

Its sandstone rock formations were among its biggest draws.

There were acres and acres of flat land to build whatever movie set they wanted.

One of the biggest filmed product to come out of the area, was Shirley Temple's most successful movie.

It was called, *Wee Willie Winkle*, and it was filmed around

1938 and the movie sets were centered in the very center of the ex-potato growing area.

Even while one movie was filming in the area, it never stopped other film makers from doing their thing just over the next hill and out of sight of each other.

Shooting the Westerns were very big in those days and one film production company always had to tell the others in the area when gunfire was going to be used. This was done so that. they could stop their camera from rolling until the noise· stopped and was no danger to the film they were doing picking up the sounds.

There was always filming going on in the area.

The Iverson family hired professionals to oversee each production and supervise who had permission to be on what piece of land at certain time schedules.

All of these things allowed the family Iverson, to roll in some major money and they did not have to do anything to earn it.

The details go something like this. The Family Iverson came to the San Fernando Valley in the late 1880's, but it wasn't until 1908 that the family got involved in the movie business.

The Following are two brief stories that are told about their humble beginnings. I also heard that there was a third story circulating but I haven't heard it yet.

The original story was that someone knocked on their door and explained that they wished to use their land for a Hollywood Film that they were shooting. They were looking for some background shots for their action sequences.

And since the family had no experience in these matters, they agreed to a daily rental fee of five dollars.

Then another film company came by and the family knew that they had to get ready to enter "the game."

The second interesting story found the family discovering a film company using their land without their permission.

After a heavy discussion with the unwanted guests, the film company made them an offer they did not refuse, and the family was off and running into this new business that would make them all rich but not famous.

On a personal note, I decided to check out the area myself and see what I could.

In a book about big budget movies, I read about a movie set for an Egyptian Time Line. They had a huge set with large statues sitting on familiar looking rock formations and I wanted to see if this report was accurate since this area was my own.

I was determined to see the area they used for myself. That is if I could find it.

You see, there was some confusion for me because they had built a lot of condo's all around the original sites. So, I parked my car in the local residence parking lot, and I was on my way to having my own very private adventure.

I walked down a path between condos and climbed over a fence meant to keep most wildlife out.

As I walked about, I noticed several spots that seemed familiar to me.

There was a lot of brush and trees, but taking them away in my 'minds' eye' and I had an area that was used in several scenes from the "Bonanza T V Show as well as others.

As I continued, I couldn't help but look into the past history of television and cinema in the area.

Suddenly I came to what some might call a cliff. There was a huge drop off into a long narrow valley below and then the rocks would show up again.

I knew instantly that this was one of the areas where, 'Wee Willie Winkle' was filmed. But there was also something else that caught my attention.

By my feet, imbedded in the ground, was a half circle of what appeared to be at first glance, railroad tracks.

Then it struck me. This was where a camera was mounted on these rails designed for it to be mobile.

They left them in the ground because it must have been so hard to install them, that they didn't want to take the time to remove them.

It was probably better to leave them where they were in case they should return for a re-shoot or something.

In the 1960's, the State of California authorized construction for a freeway to connect the upper San Fernando Valley to Simi Valley.

Over the passing years, nothing about the location made the news until it was discovered that Charles Manson had stayed in an area on the property.

In 1969, he became famous for the 'Tate-La-Bianca murders. As of this date, he is still in prison waiting to die of old age.

In 1982, Joe Iverson had sold the ranch to Robert Sherman who broke up the huge estate and sold off the lower end of the filming empire.

The upper part was already closed off from the freeway going north to the fancy mansions that were being built.

The western town which was a fixture on the Iverson property turned into a mobile home park.

If you're headed for the freeway on Topanga Canyon Blvd., you can easily see the mobile homes.

It is very sad that what was once the great reminder of the old west, was now a dumpy trailer park.

Fortunately, the ranch house and the property of the original Iverson's still stands and is occupied. But the Iverson family is long gone.

In 1947 on the Western Street at the Iverson property, the crews build a permanent and complete building known as the Town Church.

For the next few years it was turned into The Western School House with interiors and exteriors that were camera ready.

For a few years, it went back to being a Church with all its fine furnishings.

Then suddenly the entire Church building was there no longer and no one admits to knowing where it went. This was somewhere around the years 1947 to 1949. May it rest in peace.

Now, let us take a moment and venture back to 1938 when the studios were making the movie 'Stagecoach', which was a breakout film for John Wayne.

This was his movie from start to finish.

One of the most famous Western scenes ever shot, was when he stood his ground and got the stagecoach to pull up and stop so that he could join the happy passengers.

Movie Producer John Ford, filmed it beautifully. He had done many movies with John Wayne and would continue that tradition for years and years.

If you've seen this movie called *Stagecoach*, then you should recall the scene I am talking about where John Wayne's character stops the stage and heaves his saddle onto the mighty coach. But in the background of what was supposed to be 'Monument Valley Arizona', a most famous location, you are really seeing 'good old Chatsworth California which was part of the original Iverson Ranch.

A few other interesting Iverson Ranch facts are that D. W. Griffith's film called "Man's Genesis" was filmed in 1912 at Iverson Ranch, as was the following year with another D. W. Griffith film called "The Squaw Man."

And finally, when I drive up Topanga Canyon Blvd. towards the freeway, I sometimes see motion picture trucks parked off to the side of the road.

This is usually around the "Rocky Peak" exit.

Of course, I don't know what they are filming there. I'm just happy to see them still doing "their thing" at the old Iverson ranch location.

Thanks for the read.
Ron Sellz

http://www.gabbyhayes.org/miscellaneous/movie_locations/iverson/images/iverson_17.jpg   8/28/2016

What WAS then And what IS Now.
    Not exActly progress

http://www.gabbyhayes.org/miscellaneous/movie_locations/iverson/images/stagecoach.jpg   8/28/2016

A SCENE FROM "StageCoach", with John Wayne

http://www.gabbyhayes.org/miscellaneous/movie_locations/iverson/images/iverson_21.jpg   8/28/2016

Apache Wells relay station in "John Waynes", "Stagecoach"

http://www.gabbyhayes.org/miscellaneous/movie_locations/iverson/images/iverson_61.jpg   8/28/2016

The CAMERAS Still Roll but, turn their back on what some say is progress. There are still a lot of areas that progress hasn't ruined.

http://www.gabbyhayes.org/miscellaneous/movie_locations/iverson/images/iverson_49.jpg   8/28/2016

In The Foreground on the right we see Rocky Peak. Now a national Park popular park for used by hikers and Rock climbers, its been in hundreds of TV shows and Movies. IF you look close you can see Hwy 27 or Topanga Canyon Blvd which goes up to the simi Valley Valley Freeway.

http://www.gabbyhayes.org/miscellaneous/movie_locations/iverson/images/iverson_43.jpg   8/28/2016

To the left we see A white sound wall to protect the homes in the gated community. The Simi Freeway runs alongside the Sound wall. That area of million Dollar homes used to be the upper End of the Iverson Ranch

http://www.gabbyhayes.org/miscellaneous/movie_locations/iverson/images/iverson_33.jpg   8/28/2016

The CALVARY is Coming and So are the Condominiums
1880's   1980's

ABOUT THE AUTHOR

When Ron was at Hanna-Barbera studios, he was the writer for *Scooby-Doo*, as well as *The Smurfs*, the *Snorks* and other well known cartoon shows. He also worked on *Mork and Mindy* and *The Pink Panther* where he made his reputation! Norman Lear›s production company put Ron to work on *Good Times*, *The Jefferson's*, *All in the Family* and *Chips*.

Danny Simon, the brother of Neil Simon later brought Ron onto his staff to write for his ABC Special. Neil Simon reportedly always said that it was his brother that taught him to write.

During his free time from all the busy creations that he worked on in Hollywood, Ron took the time to write the Thriller movie called *Terror in Paradise*. It is still available on Amazon. Also available on DaDons's Rare Laser Discs website and eBay.

Ron often talks about Bud Abbott from the team of *Abbott and Costello*. When Ron was 16 years old and living in Encino, California, he struck up a friendship with Abbott as he sat at the feet of the master, both as a friend and as a student of comedy writing.

Ron also worked with Sherwood Schwartz, the great writer and producer, over the years. With Sherwood, Ron worked on the *Gilligan's Island* series for Metro Media. Ron said that each day was so very exciting for him as he watched the characters delivering his written lines for them.

Ron's beloved characters were Gilligan, The Skipper, Mary Ann, Mrs. Howell and the Professor. Two of Ron's favorite stories include his interaction with John Travolta and Wayne Newton.

Hollywood Friends can be found on www.lostagepublishing.com. Ron is also the author of two other books, *Pickled*, and *Bound 4 Vegas*.

Ron Sellz resides in Chatsworth, CA, is happily married to his wife Teri, and has three sons: Stuart, Scott and Brandon.

www.ingramcontent.com/pod-product-compliance
Lightning Source LLC
Chambersburg PA
CBHW022012090426

42741CB00007B/993

* 9 7 8 1 9 4 6 4 8 0 0 3 3 *